Academic Writing and Plagiarism

BLOOMSBURY CLASSICS IN LINGUISTICS

Multimodal Teaching and Learning, Gunther Kress, Carey Jewitt, Jon Ogborn and Charalampos Tsatsarelis
Opposition in Discourse, Lesley Jeffries
Second Language Identities, David Block
Teacher Cognition and Language Education, Simon Borg
Worlds of Written Discourse, Vijay Bhatia

Academic Writing and Plagiarism

A linguistic analysis

DIANE PECORARI

Bloomsbury Academic
An imprint of Bloomsbury Publishing Plc

BLOOMSBURY
LONDON · NEW DELHI · NEW YORK · SYDNEY

Bloomsbury Academic
An imprint of Bloomsbury Publishing Plc

50 Bedford Square 1385 Broadway
London New York
WC1B 3DP NY 10018
UK USA

www.bloomsbury.com

BLOOMSBURY and the Diana logo are trademarks of Bloomsbury Publishing Plc

First published 2008

Bloomsbury Classics in Linguistics edition first published in 2015 by Bloomsbury Academic

© Diane Pecorari 2008, 2015

Diane Pecorari has asserted her right under the Copyright, Designs and Patents Act, 1988, to be identified as Author of this work.

All rights reserved. No part of this publication may be reproduced or transmitted in any form or by any means, electronic or mechanical, including photocopying, recording, or any information storage or retrieval system, without prior permission in writing from the publishers.

No responsibility for loss caused to any individual or organization acting on or refraining from action as a result of the material in this publication can be accepted by Bloomsbury or the author.

British Library Cataloguing-in-Publication Data
A catalogue record for this book is available from the British Library.

ISBN: PB: 978-1-4725-8910-1
ePDF: 978-1-4742-5462-5
ePub: 978-1-4725-8920-0

Library of Congress Cataloging-in-Publication Data
A catalog record for this book is available from the Library of Congress

Series: Bloomsbury Classics in Linguistics

Typeset by Deanta Global Publishing Services, Chennai, India

For Chiara and Lucia

Contents

Acknowledgements viii

1 Plagiarism: Why the need for a linguistic analysis? 1
2 Plagiarism in perspective 9
3 Learning to write from sources 37
4 The texts 57
5 'My position, it is impossible': The writers' perspectives 99
6 The readers 125
7 Plagiarism, patchwriting and source use in context 145

Appendix: Research method 171
References 191
Author Index 209
Subject Index 213

Acknowledgements

This book is in part about intertextual relationships and the ways they are signalled, so it is only appropriate to begin it by acknowledging some of the important influences on this text. Maggie Charles offered insightful comments which greatly strengthened the rigour and the readability of the finished product and has been an encouraging force since the early days of this project. Martin Hewings, Diane Belcher and Malcolm Coulthard have contributed in important ways to my understanding of plagiarism in academic writing. Karin Molander Danielsson has been generous with her time in reading, listening to and commenting on my approaches to the ideas presented here. Chiara Pecorari has allowed me to share in her acquisition of academic literacy, and has been a sunny presence throughout the writing of this book. I am grateful to all of them for the contributions they have made to this book.

1

Plagiarism: Why the need for a linguistic analysis?

The overarching purpose of this book is to examine plagiarism as a linguistic phenomenon, rather than as a violation of rules or ethical principles. While it is true that plagiarism *is* a violation of the rules governing conduct in many circumstances (for instance, university classrooms), and of widely held ethical principles, it is also an act of language use. If to plagiarize is to 'take (the work or an idea of someone else) and pass it off as one's own', as the *Concise Oxford English Dictionary* says, then the 'passing off' occurs when the work or idea is articulated by the person who took it. The plagiarism is not complete until the 'taker' writes or speaks about the work or idea, identifying it as his or her own. Plagiarism is, therefore, fundamentally a specific kind of language in use, a linguistic phenomenon.

The linguistics of plagiarism have, however, generally been overlooked, just as the immorality of it has been proclaimed frequently, and in scathing terms. 'To take a piece of writing without acknowledging the creator is plain theft' (Ragen, 1987, p. A39) was the verdict of an academic commenting on a case of plagiarism that attracted public attention. While the case that provoked the comment was controversial, the identification of plagiarism with theft is not at all so; stealing is a common metaphor for plagiarism.

In keeping with the metaphor of theft, the received view is that plagiarism is not only a flaw in the text in which it occurs, but also a threat to other texts, and to the discourse communities which produce them. Plagiarism in science 'subverts [scientists'] own achievement' (Klein, 1993, p. S57); one editor of a scholarly journal commented,

> Incidents of plagiarism in science corrupt the soul of the perpetrator... Erode the integrity of the discipline, and diminish the esteem of science in the minds of the general public. If plagiarism in science were allowed to become widespread, science would ultimately be destroyed.
> (Betts, 1992, p. 289)

These comments, typical of the discourse surrounding plagiarism, illustrate how the act is cast in moral terms, and that the effects of the 'corruption' are seen to reach beyond the texts which are immediately involved. Consequently, the treatment accorded to plagiarism is very different from the response to other flawed aspects of a text.

This special treatment is evidenced by the language of prevention used to discuss the act in student writing. Handbooks for teachers, detection software packages and materials directed at students all speak of 'preventing plagiarism'. Since plagiarism is an undesirable textual feature, the emphasis on prevention may seem reasonable, yet other undesirable textual features are approached differently. Instead of *preventing poor paragraphing* or *preventing an unfocused text* or *preventing subject-verb disagreement* teachers try to *promote* good argumentation, organization and lexico-grammatical choices. While other aspects of writing are judged on a cline of more or less successful performance, plagiarism is judged on another dimension entirely. The opposite of poor organization is effective organization, something that makes a text stronger. The opposite of plagiarism is the absence of plagiarism, a neutral feature. The absence of plagiarism does not guarantee that sources have been used effectively, but simply that a text lacks what would otherwise be a serious flaw.

When presented to novice writers, plagiarism is again treated differently from other writing issues. Writing is a skill, and writing from sources[1] is an important subskill for academic writers, yet the instructions students receive about plagiarism are often in the form of warnings and information sheets emphasizing declarative knowledge about the act, rather than the skills needed to avoid it. When the warnings have been delivered, the responsibility for plagiarism is assigned firmly to the student; it is assumed that a student who has been told not to plagiarize and still does so has either failed to be sufficiently attentive to instructions or deliberately stepped outside the framework of the rules. Plagiarism is traditionally constructed not as a failure to write well, but as a refusal to engage legitimately in the writing process at all.

However, more recently an alternative understanding of plagiarism has challenged this received view. The first- and second-language composition literature has featured a number of accounts of apparent plagiarism appearing in circumstances which make it difficult to portray the writer as a run-of-the-mill plagiarist. An early example comes from Carolyn Matalene's (1985) paper calling for awareness of contrastive rhetoric in teaching non-native speakers of English (NNSEs). She illustrated the need for contrastive rhetorical awareness by recounting an experience with a class in China. After reading an autobiographical piece by Anaïs Nin, Matalene's students were set the task of writing about their own lives. When the students borrowed chunks of the model text, Matalene confronted them with what she viewed as their unacceptable conduct. A discussion ensued, during which the students argued that they had written the way they had been taught to. Afterwards, one of the students summarized the episode like this:

> After our teacher's explanation, we understand that in her country or some others plagiarism is forbidden. . . . However in our country, things are [a] little different. We may perhaps call what our teacher calls 'plagiarism' as 'imitation', which is sometimes encouraged, especially for a beginner.
>
> (1985, p. 803)

Similar in many respects are the accounts of student writers at a South African university in Angélil-Carter's (2000) study. One of the writers, Bulelwa, had had limited exposure to English before beginning university, and this created a dilemma for her as she tried to write from sources. She understood the need not to plagiarize, but did not feel confident about her ability to do so without misrepresenting her sources. In response to these conflicting concerns, she developed a hybrid strategy: 'if I want something to be clearer, sometimes I use his [the source's] words sometimes I use mine'. Despite her concern about accuracy, she tried to paraphrase, saying 'by paraphrasing it I don't want to plagiarize' (p. 96). However, Bulelwa's efforts were not successful in the view of her tutor, who categorized her work as plagiarism (p. 95).

In both of these episodes, typical of many others described in the literature[2], a key issue is intention. Both Bulelwa and the Chinese writers copied language from their sources, but in neither case does it appear that their intention was to practice deception in order to gain unearned credit for work that was not theirs. In the case of the students in China, this is shown most forcefully by the fact that the source they copied from was one that their teacher had assigned them to read, and could therefore be expected to recognize. Bulelwa articulated a strategy of consciously trying to avoid the pitfall of plagiarism, while simultaneously attending to another aspect of good writing, presenting ideas from sources in an accurate way. Nonetheless, in both cases what the students produced was called plagiarism by their teachers. There appear, therefore, to be at least two sorts of plagiarism, distinguished by the presence or absence of intentional deception. Here the term *prototypical plagiarism* will be used to refer to the former, and will be defined as

> the use of words and/or ideas from another source, without appropriate attribution, and with the intention to deceive.

Demonstrating intentional deception is not straightforward, though, and in certain cases it may be questionable whether deceptive intent was present, but hard to determine conclusively that it was not. It is therefore necessary to be able to discuss plagiarism without reference to intent, taking into account only the textual features, i.e., the similarity of one text to another, and the absence of other textual features, such as quotation marks, which would make the similarity acceptable. Here the term *textual plagiarism* will be used and defined like this:

> Textual plagiarism is the use of words and/or ideas from another source, without appropriate attribution.

Finally, as already noted, a type of plagiarism exists which is characterized by the lack of deceptive intent. Often the language from one or more source texts is not only adopted, but also woven into the student's text, mixed with parts that have been written more autonomously; it shows signs of having been adapted to the new text: synonyms have been substituted, active verbs made passive or vice versa and so on. This source use strategy is what Rebecca Howard (1995, 1999) calls *patchwriting,* and defines as 'copying from a source text and then deleting some words, altering grammatical structures, or plugging in one synonym for another' (1999, p. xvii). Patchwriting, according to Howard, is virtually inevitable as writers learn to produce texts within a new discourse community, and is a beneficial part of the learning process,

> a primary means of understanding difficult texts, of expanding one's lexical, stylistic, and conceptual repertoires, of finding and trying out new voices in which to speak.
>
> (1999, p. xviii)

Patchwriting gives writers the chance to flex their muscles under controlled and guided circumstances—guided by the linguistic choices of the source authors.

Patchwriting comes about as a result of novice writers' need for support as they develop, and not because the writer intends to deceive the reader. Patchwriting and prototypical plagiarism can therefore be seen as subcategories of textual plagiarism, distinguished by the presence or absence of intention to deceive (Figure 1.1) A further reason for the need of a linguistic analysis of plagiarism can now

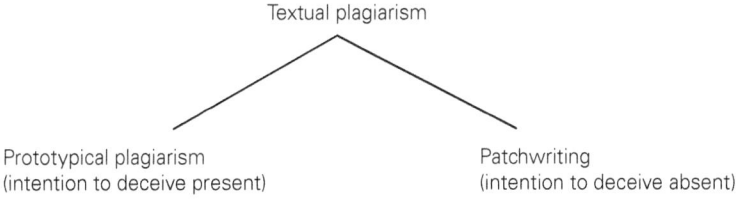

FIGURE 1.1 *Types of plagiarism.*

be seen: one type of plagiarism, patchwriting, is a byproduct of the process of learning to write in a new context. It is, therefore, one aspect of language learning.

Yet another set of reasons relates to the criteria for establishing that either type of textual plagiarism exists. To determine that a piece of writing contains textual plagiarism, three things must be true. First, the new text must contain words and/or ideas that are also present in an earlier text. In principle, plagiarism could involve the appropriation of ideas expressed entirely in new language; however, in practice, it is often the similarity of language that arouses suspicion and serves as evidence of plagiarism. The linguistic relationship between two texts is, therefore, an important element.

Secondly, to meet the definition of textual plagiarism, a new text must *repeat* words or ideas from an earlier one; that is, the similarity between two texts cannot be coincidental. This is one reason why those in the position of trying to determine whether plagiarism has occurred—for example, teachers or members of disciplinary boards—take length into account. The longer the chunks of language that two texts share, intuition suggests, the greater the likelihood that plagiarism has occurred. If it were possible to be certain that similarities between two texts were entirely coincidental, the label *plagiarism* would not be applied to it. Writing processes are, therefore, a key to understanding plagiarism.

The third and final criterion is that the new text must fail to attribute its relationship to an earlier one, or fail to attribute it adequately. Quotation, for example, involves the intentional repetition of language in a prior text, but provided that quotation marks are in place and the source is cited, plagiarism is not involved. However, whether attribution is adequate is not determined by absolute principles; among the factors that must be taken into account are the reader's understanding and the conventional expectations of the discourse community in which the text is produced. Textual plagiarism, therefore, results not only from writing processes, but is partially constructed by the reader (an idea which will be explored in a later chapter).

An examination of plagiarism as a matter of ethical concern involves looking at a particular set of intertextual relationships in the context of rules and standards. A full understanding of plagiarism requires going deeper still, and examining the nature of the intertextual relationship itself. The purpose of this book is to provide such a detailed examination of the linguistic aspects of plagiarism, by presenting the findings of an investigation into the source use of 17 writers.

Plagiarism is an issue in a wide range of areas: journalism, politics and literature are just a few of the fields in which high-profile cases of plagiarism regularly appear. The context in which it occurs makes a great deal of difference, though, to a number of specific questions, so this study concentrates on a single context: plagiarism and source use in academic writing, and specifically in the writing of postgraduate students. The 17 postgraduates whose work is studied here are all NNSEs. This criterion was built into the research design not through a belief that NNSEs are greatly more likely to plagiarize than native speakers (see Chapter 2 for a discussion of this question), but because language skills, as noted above, are deeply implicated in plagiarism, and therefore are likely to play a role in the specifics of the act. Because context, again, is important, the writers were drawn from four academic areas: the social sciences, the humanities, engineering and natural sciences.

The next chapter reviews several ideas closely implicated in plagiarism. Chapter 3 consists of a more detailed exposition of the contextual factors mentioned above: the role of citation in academic texts, the expectations of the discourse community and the processes of learning to write from sources. Chapters 4, 5 and 6 will look at the source use of the 17 students from three different perspectives: the texts, the writers and their readers. The final chapter will discuss the implications of these findings within the university.

Notes

1   Russ Hunt has pointed out (in a personal communication, 7 September 2007) that 'writing from sources' suggests a mechanical, repetitive process, while what experienced academic writers do—or at least try to do—is engage with sources and use them for a purpose. For reasons of efficiency I will use the expression 'writing from sources' here, but will use it to mean writing which draws on sources in that fuller and more meaningful way.

2 See, for example, Braine (1995), Connor and Kramer (1995), Crocker and Shaw (2002), Dong (1998), Leki (1995), McClanahan (2005), Pecorari (2003), Petrić (2004), Prior (1998), Shaw (1991), Sherman (1992), Spack (1997) and St. John (1987) for evidence of students producing writing which is, or is likely to be, judged as plagiarism by their teachers, but who appear not to have intended to be deceptive.

2

Plagiarism in perspective

Why do writers plagiarize? Sometimes they are dishonest and are willing to break the rules, of which they are quite aware, in order to gain unearned benefit. Another reason can be simple necessity. In a study of the progress of a second-language writer through a business course, Currie (1998) found that the student, Diana, worked diligently in the early weeks of the course to raise the level of her writing assignments, but was at real risk of not receiving the grade she needed to stay in her program. Eventually Diana hit upon the strategy of repeating words and phrases from her sources; in other words, she began to patchwrite. From then on her teacher's feedback was more positive. Although Diana adopted the patchwriting strategy consciously, she differed from the prototypical plagiarist in at least two important respects. First, unlike a student who buys an essay from the internet and thus gains credit without expending effort, Diana's patchwriting cost her substantial time and energy. Currie notes that

> It is difficult to read the juxtaposed texts without realizing the extraordinary time, effort, and patience it must have taken for Diana to struggle through the reading, find precisely those phrases or sentences that met her needs in terms of content and generality, and then weave them together, using still-developing syntactic skills, into what she hoped would bring her an acceptable grade.
>
> (1998, p. 9)

In addition, there is no indication that Diana saw her strategy as cheating; in contrast, she described it as a positive approach to learning the specialist terminology of her area, as her teacher had encouraged her to (p. 10).

Another (closely related) cause of plagiarism may be the lack of awareness that certain writing strategies may be considered inappropriate. This was what Matalene's Chinese students, quoted in Chapter 1, argued: 'we may perhaps call what our teacher calls "plagiarism" as "imitation," which is sometimes encouraged, especially for a beginner' (1985, p. 803). Supporting this explanation is a certain amount of research showing that some students do not perceive as inappropriate some forms of intertextuality which their teachers are likely to object to (e.g. Deckert, 1993; Errey, 2002; Hayes and Introna, 2005).

These three explanations amount to saying that writers may plagiarize as an act of intentional wrongdoing; or because they are attending to another objective (such as learning the terminology of their area) and lose sight of source-use issues; or because they do not know that certain writing strategies are labelled plagiarism and considered wrong. What these explanations have in common is that they hinge on a deficit in the writer. Writers plagiarize because they are in some way unwilling or unable to use sources in appropriate ways. The last of the three, though, can be framed in another way. Instead of saying that plagiarism can happen because writers do not know what acts fall under the heading of plagiarism, it is equally possible to say that textual plagiarism can be identified when student writers and the people who evaluate their work do not agree about which kinds of source use are appropriate. That is, the problem may not be that one group has a mistaken perception, but that two groups have different perceptions.

This reformulation shifts the potential wrongness of a particular kind of intertextual relationship from the individuals involved to the context in which texts are produced and read. The importance of considering textual plagiarism in context is a theme that recurs in the coming chapters. The remainder of this chapter illustrates this by considering plagiarism from four specific perspectives. The next section presents a brief review of the historical development of the concept of plagiarism. The following section examines plagiarism in intercultural educational contexts, and the final two sections explore two very public episodes of plagiarism.

Plagiarism in Historical Context

The word *plagiarism* itself has origins in antiquity, and its negative associations stretch back as far: 'the derivation from the Latin word meaning "kidnap" or "plunder" is indicative of how since its first usage in this way it has been regarded as a criminal activity—parallel to stealing other people's offspring!' (Angélil-Carter, 2000, pp. 16–17). Plagiarism in its modern sense, though, could not exist without the closely related ideas of copyright and intellectual property, the initial development of which, in the fifteenth century, was contemporary with that of the printing press. This innovation allowed texts to circulate more widely and profitably, and raised two perennially relevant questions: Who should control the distribution of texts? and who should profit from them?

A landmark event in intellectual property law came in England in 1557 when the Stationer's Company, a trade organization of book sellers, was granted a Royal Charter, giving it the ability effectively to authorize the publication of books. Financial benefits from this arrangement accrued to the stationers, while the monarch obtained the stationers' services as censors, an important advantage, 'for with the coming of print to the West at the end of the fifteenth century, both Church and State had reason to fear the proliferation of blasphemous or seditious ideas' (Baron, 2000, p. 59).

At this point the author was a marginal figure, and the rights in and benefits from publications accrued to those who produced and sold books. The adage that freedom of the press applies only to those who own one was fully relevant throughout the sixteenth century. With the coming of the Enlightenment, though, this began to change. Locke established that the act of creation was implicated in the ownership of property, a cornerstone in the concept of authorship and authors' rights (Baron, 2000; Halbert, 1999; Howard, 1999).

The next development, and according to Howard the 'most significant for the place of plagiarism in intellectual hierarchy today is the premise that the writer is capable of producing an original text, one of a kind. This premise was supplied energetically by a succession of eighteenth- and nineteenth-century writers' (1999, p. 92). It is no coincidence, then, that copyright laws assigning rights and benefits to the author began to appear in this period. In 1710 the Statute of Queen Anne gave authors a copyright for a period of 14 years. Subsequent Copyright Acts were passed in 1814 and 1842, the latter extending the period of protection to 42 years, or 7 years *postmortem auctoris* (Baron, 2000). Lobbying for these changes were prominent literary names with familiar financial motives:

> In an effort to live by the pen, to promote their own writing in a market awash in printed matter, Romantic poets from Herder and Goethe to Wordsworth and Coleridge tended to emphasize the element of innovation in composition—to stress their break with tradition to create something utterly new, unique—in a word, 'original.'
>
> (Woodmansee and Jaszi, 1995, p. 769)

The trend in copyright law since has been increasing inclusivity about what uses violate copyright, and longer copyright periods (Woodmansee and Jaszi, 1995).

The view of plagiarism as an infringement on the rights of the author rests, therefore, on a view of the rights of the author which arose in a particular sociohistorical context (Pennycook, 1994, 1996; Scollon, 1994, 1995). Plagiarism is not a violation of an absolute standard; it is the product of a particular context and cannot be judged without reference to the context in which it occurs.

Plagiarism in Intercultural Context

A received view among many teachers who work with international students is that such students are especially likely to plagiarize. So entrenched is this idea that one paper on plagiarism begins with the simple assertion that 'one obvious cause [of increased plagiarism] is the influx of foreign students into engineering fields'(Brogan and Brogan, 1983, p. 4). The numerous accounts of textual plagiarism involving NNSEs in the composition literature have contributed to this view, and there has been considerable speculation about why this might be the case. Attempts at explanation have included the following assertions[1].

- Students from a 'collectivist' culture may not perceive a need to give credit to individual authors.
- Ideas can be owned, and therefore need to be cited, is not a common belief in all cultures.
- A desire to preserve social harmony may make it difficult to attach criticism to individual authors.
- Students' perceptions about their roles, e.g. a belief that their role as writers is to repeat information from sources, may make them feel that citations are superfluous.
- Writers may perceive that there is a single correct truth, and believe therefore that *where* a fact comes from is unimportant.
- A textual tradition in which a few widely read canonical texts have great importance may make citations seem superfluous, since the reader and the writer can be assumed to have a shared knowledge of the source of ideas. Indeed, a citation may seem potentially offensive if it suggests that the reader—the teacher—would not recognize the texts that were used.
- Experience with memorization and rote learning may lead to reproductive writing strategies.
- Understanding what is common knowledge and thus does not need to be cited can be problematic.
- Finally, it has even been asserted that in some cultures plagiarism is not a relevant concept, or not conceived of in the same way as it is in the West.

These ideas have proven appealing to many teachers, partly because they are quite plausible. So many important differences exist between cultures as diverse as, say, China and the United States, that it is not difficult to imagine the differences influencing the way sources are referred to in academic texts. Another source of their appeal is that they provide an explanation for occurrences of student plagiarism which are more palatable than the alternative, that the student set out to cheat. Yet as Buranen (1999) points out, these culture-based explanations have gained currency in much the same way as urban myths do:

> although no one has ever actually blown up a cat in the microwave or eaten a Big Mac made of ground worms, many people have a 'friend of a friend' who has. . . . In this case, no one I talked to had heard directly from an Asian student that his copying from the text was a form of respect for the received wisdom of his ancestors or from a Middle-Eastern student that her family were only trying to help her graduate, but many seemed to have a 'friend of a friend' who had.
>
> (p. 67)

A study of both student and staff accounts of plagiarism (Errey, 2002) endorses this; while the staff offered explanations like the ones above for international student plagiarism, students themselves did not believe that culture was a factor. Insider accounts have also cast doubts upon cultural explanations. When an article appeared in the *ELT Journal* enumerating possible cultural factors which could cause plagiarism (Sowden, 2005a), responses followed from two academics, one from China and one from Vietnam (Ha, 2006; Liu, 2005), arguing forcefully that plagiarism is not condoned in their countries, and suggesting that possible cultural differences have been overstated. According to Liu,

> even in ancient China . . . people were required to credit their sources. For instance, if one quoted Confucius, one had to say 'Zi [a short name for Confucius] yue [said]. . .', . . . (Thus the claim that Chinese usually quote Confucius or other famous scholars without mentioning their source is inaccurate.) Again, I am not suggesting

that Chinese always cite their sources in such cases. They do not, yet do English speakers sometimes not do the same when they cite in their speeches well-known quotes such as J. F. Kennedy's 'Ask not what your country can do for you, ask . . . ,' Churchill's 'blood, sweat, and tears,' and many of Benjamin Franklin's axioms?
(2005, p. 236)

Similarly, an interview study found that 'plagiarism both exists and is recognizable in Chinese academic life' (Bloch, 2001, p. 217), while another study (Bloch and Chi, 1995) concluded that 'taking a critical position seems to be considered an acceptable and important part of Chinese academic writing' (p. 257).

What can be concluded is that while explanations for plagiarism based on cultural differences may be appealing, there is reason to be sceptical of them. A small but growing body of empirical research has addressed two related questions: are non-native speakers of English more likely to plagiarize than native speakers? and what are the causes of plagiarism in the writing of NNSEs? A small body of research to date has sought an answer to the first question from textual evidence. Campbell (1990) conducted an experimental investigation into the source use strategies of NESs (native English speakers) and NNSEs. Students were assigned a text to read and then to write on a related topic. Some differences between the NES and NNSE groups were found, including the fact that the NNSEs were more reliant on the background text in the initial part of their writing samples. Interestingly, for all students the body of the essay contained less material from the source and the conclusion more. Campbell concluded that language proficiency was the cause of the difference, and that 'cultural differences did not seem to explain the results in this study' (1990, p. 225).

Shi (2004) also used experimental conditions to test for possible differences between Chinese and North American students. She found that the Chinese students repeated more language from their sources on a task that asked them to summarize, but that the differences between groups disappeared when they wrote on a topic which required them to put forth an opinion. On both tasks the English speakers were more likely to provide a reference in conjunction with language from the source. Howard (2007) looked at source use in the authentic writing of undergraduates in the United States. Although she did not control for first language, the writers in her sample came from a course which enrolls primarily English L1 speakers. Comparing her findings to earlier ones based on NNSEs (Pecorari, 2003), Howard concluded that while her writers repeated shorter chunks of language from their sources, they were equally likely to obscure the relationship between their texts and their sources.

The relative frequency of textual plagiarism in NNSE and NES writing has also been investigated indirectly, through students' self-reports on questionnaires. Rinnert and Kobayashi (2005) found that Japanese and American students reported using language from their sources, but that a much higher proportion of American students said they were always or usually careful to 'give credit' in such cases (92.2 per cent versus 55.4 per cent; for the 'always' category alone the figures were 70.1 per cent versus 18.5 per cent), although it is not clear whether by 'give credit' the students meant only citing the source, or enclosing repeated language in quotation marks as well.

Hayes and Introna (2005) asked four groups of students—Asian, Chinese, Greek and British—whether they had 'copied a paragraph or more word for word once or more' or 'copied a few sentences word for word once or more' (p. 219). Not surprisingly, in all groups a higher proportion of students reported copying shorter chunks of text than longer ones. Differences were also found across national groups, but the differences are difficult to interpret in terms of NES versus NNSE backgrounds. The Chinese, Greek and British students reported having copied a few sentences equally frequently (56, 57 and 56 per cent of students, respectively, said they had done this), while 75 per cent of the Asian students said they had done so. When it came to copying longer chunks, between 19 and 21 per cent of the Asian, Greek and British students reported having copied paragraph-length or longer chunks, while 40 per cent of the Chinese students had done so.

What can be concluded from these studies? Differences have indeed been found between NES students and (some) groups of NNSEs. However, the differences appear not to be primarily related to the likelihood of students committing textual plagiarism, but to the qualitative aspects of their source use. The nature of the writing task and the section in which sources are used both appear to be factors (and possibly related ones, to the extent that introductions often create a background for the topic by summarizing what other writers have said about it) and the permissible length of borrowed strings. At present, therefore, it is not clear that textual plagiarism occurs more often in the writing of NNSEs, but there is reason to think that it may occur in different ways.

If so, what are the reasons for this? The results of several questionnaire studies suggest that (some) NNSEs do not identify some kinds of source use as plagiarism, while more established members of the academic discourse community—their teachers for example—would. A survey of Hong Kong university students asked them to identify appropriate and inappropriate source use in six writing samples (Deckert, 1993). Two of the samples were designed to reflect fully appropriate source use and the other four to reflect varying degrees of inappropriateness. The 170 first-year students surveyed were not able to make this identification reliably: just over 20 per cent said the two 'appropriate' samples represented the worst example of plagiarism, while the two examples intended to be least appropriate were labelled as fully acceptable by 20 per cent and 37 per cent of the students, respectively. Deckert concluded that lack of knowledge about plagiarism and attitudes at odds with Western values accounted for these findings. It seems equally possible, though, that methodological difficulties may provide at least a partial explanation for the results. The task the participants were asked to complete (and this was only one part of a longer questionnaire) required, among other things, close attention to six texts and the ability to imagine the source use exemplified in real-life contexts; those are high expectations to have of a large group of young university students undertaking a task that offered no incentive for careful contributions.

Attitude differences were also found in the two survey studies referred to above. In Rinnert and Kobayashi's (2005) survey of Japanese and American students, the Japanese students were far less negative towards plagiarism; indeed, a majority thought it was acceptable under some conditions at least. The conditions under which they thought plagiarism might be acceptable were both practical (some said plagiarism 'cannot be helped') and contextual ('okay for a report' or 'as long as the ideas are fully understood') (p. 39). Among the American group, though, only 5 per cent were prepared to accept plagiarism as acceptable in any circumstances, and the majority gave as their reason for objecting to it that 'it was unethical or resulted from laziness, or both' (p. 39). Two points are worth noting here. The first is that, as the authors themselves note, there is a potential methodological problem in that the word for plagiarism used in the Japanese survey, *ukeuri*, does not have precisely the same connotations as the English word. Second, by objecting to plagiarism in conditional terms, rather than with blanket moral condemnation, the Japanese students may have been reflecting an understanding of textual plagiarism as the complex phenomenon it really is. In other words, they may not have been demonstrating a different set of ethical values but merely a more sophisticated understanding of the concept.

The groups of students surveyed by Hayes and Introna (2005) not only differed in terms of how often they reported having copied from sources, but also in how seriously they regarded such copying. Copying a paragraph or more was viewed as serious cheating by a majority of all students, but by a smaller majority of Asian and Chinese students (60 and 70 per cent, respectively) than Greek (93 per cent) and British (75 per cent). Copying smaller chunks ('a few sentences') was considered serious cheating by similar proportions of British, Greek and Chinese students (38, 36, and 40 per cent, respectively), but by none of the Asian students.

There is, therefore, some support for the idea that at least some groups of NNSEs may differ from NESs in terms of the intertextual relationships they consider acceptable, but reason to be sceptical of simple relationships, such as 'students from *X* do not understand plagiarism'. What factors underlie these differences, such as they are?

As noted above, differences in cultural values or orientations are often given as a reason for textual plagiarism in the writing of NNSEs. To date little evidence is available to support this claim. The first-year students who answered Deckert's (1993) questionnaire said that plagiarism was wrong for reasons to do with their own learning outcomes. Comparing his findings to an earlier study of US students (Kroll, 1988), Deckert concluded that the Hong Kong students did not share the same concern for the rights of the individual author. When the questionnaire was repeated with a smaller number of third-year students, plagiarism was also characterized as 'dishonest'. Deckert interpreted this as showing that 'the two years of college experience seems to have acquainted students with the notion of respect for other persons' ownership of words and ideas' (p. 141). However, this finding should be interpreted with caution. Only four of the 170 first-year students said they had had the English word *plagiarism* explained to them before the questionnaire, so too much should not be concluded from their ability, or lack thereof, to explain why it is wrong.

In a more recent study (Shi, 2006), German, Asian and NES students were interviewed about questions related to source use and plagiarism. Fourteen of the 25 Asian students felt that words can be shared, and therefore copying can be acceptable, while 9 of the 11 English speakers said that words can become the intellectual property of an individual. Sixteen of the Asian students felt that there had been an increase in the importance placed on intellectual property rights in their home country, and that this was due to Western influence, implying that some difference in orientation towards intellectual property rights exists in Eastern and Western cultures. Fourteen of the Asian students stated that plagiarism, as understood in the English-speaking world, 'created a cultural hurdle for them' (p. 271). Only three of the German students shared this view, and then in more qualified terms: they 'felt it might be a cultural hurdle because plagiarism in German schools and universities was not treated as a crime but a problem of style' (p. 272).

That last response highlights another factor for which considerably more support is available: the educational system, which differs from country to country in terms of the extent to which the skills related to writing from sources, or indeed writing at all, are taught. In Shi's (2006) study, the majority of NES and German students had practiced citation skills in secondary schools, but only 2 of the 25 Asian students had. Similar differences in learning about citation skills were found between Japanese and American students (Rinnert and Kobayashi, 2005), and in general Japanese students have been said to receive little instruction in the schools in academic writing (Dryden, 1999; LoCastro and Masuko, 2002). The lack of writing instruction and assessed work involving writing among some groups of international students has also been documented elsewhere (Bloch, 2001;

Hayes and Introna, 2005; Timm, 2007a, 2007b). If NNSEs use citing practices which are not widely approved in the Anglophone academic discourse community, it may be because they simply do not have the same degree of practice in writing from sources as English L1 students. Another, closely related question is language ability. NNSEs writing in English have, manifestly, difficulties that NESs do not. This is not to suggest that learning to produce academic discourse is unproblematic for NESs, but that the difficulties are both qualitatively and quantitatively different for NNSEs. Reproducing strings of language is seen by some NNSEs as a coping strategy to meet the demands of producing fluent-sounding academic discourse in a foreign language (e.g. Barks and Watts, 2001; Bloch and Chi, 1995; Currie, 1998; Shi, 2006). Indeed, recycling chunks of language may be seen by L2 writers not as a necessary evil, but as a positive strategy. That was one of the findings of a groundbreaking study by Flowerdew and Li (2007), who interviewed PhD students across four disciplines and looked at their writing. Although the participants were students, most had had research articles either published or accepted for publication. They were thus playing an active role in their academic discourse communities, and one of their strategies for doing so was patchwriting. For these writers textual plagiarism was not a question of 'needs must'; it was a strategy they saw both as acceptable and beneficial. Flowerdew and Li conclude that the writers were working to this rule: 'as long as the "work" is their own, the language can be borrowed, to various extents and for various reasons, from one text into another' (pp. 459–460).

Another relevant aspect of language use is reading ability. Howard (2001) notes that one cause of patchwriting is when the writer has not fully understood the source text. In a study of US university lecturers (or professors, in US terms), Roig (2001) found that nearly a third completed a paraphrasing task based on an academic text by repeating strings of language from the source which, according to the terms of his study, were long enough to be regarded as plagiarized. However, when another group was asked to complete the same task using a simpler source, the proportion repeating equally long strings of text dropped to 3 per cent. If reading comprehension can have this effect on a group presumably composed primarily of native English speakers, it can safely be concluded that it is an even more salient issue for NNSEs.

What can be said in conclusion, then, about the relationship between L1 status and plagiarism? The evidence is compelling that textual plagiarism is not an uncommon feature in the work of NNSEs. There is reason to think, though, that the same is likely to be true for NESs. It is possible that any differences between the two groups are not in the likelihood of textual plagiarism occurring, but in quantitative features such as the length of borrowed strings and qualitative features such as the linguistic dexterity with which borrowed chunks are merged. Some groups of NNSEs are likely to have had less experience of, and training in, writing from sources, and are therefore perhaps more likely to need additional support for their writing. It is less clear that the source use practices of NNSEs can be attributed to differences in cultural values or orientations. This does not necessarily mean, though, that the notion of culture is irrelevant to questions of intertextuality. As Buranen notes,

> Assumptions about what constitutes plagiarism or 'ownership of text' may or may not be exclusively or even predominantly a matter of culture, but cultural difference can serve to further muddy some already murky waters.
>
> (1999, p. 65)

The existing data is not sufficient to permit any firm conclusions about the relationship between culture and plagiarism to be reached. There is, therefore, ample scope for continued research into this question. However, some potential risks should be borne in mind. One of these is the ever-present risk of essentializing and oversimplifying: 'cross-cultural comparison runs the danger of dichotomizing the two cultures into polar opposites, presenting one culture as the opposite of the other' (Bloch, 2001, p. 213; Buranen, 1999, makes a similar point). Where differences are identified, there is a risk of succumbing to the idea that they are something to be 'fixed', to bring NNSEs' writing practices into alignment with Western notions of intertextual propriety.

Plagiarism has been discussed as an act of resistance (Bloch, 2001; Chandrasoma et al., 2004; Pennycook, 1996), and in the context of teaching NNSEs about the standards of the Anglophone academic discourse community (Belcher and Braine, 1995), the issue becomes salient. This does not necessarily militate against researching the ways that culture can be implicated in plagiarism, or applying those lessons in the classroom. Without an awareness of what is expected, there can be no meaningful choice to 'accommodate, resist, or accommodate for the sake of resistance' (Belcher, 1997, p. 11). The issue does, however, illustrate the need for a nuanced approach to investigating the relationship between plagiarism and culture.

Plagiarism in Transatlantic Politics

In the spring of 1987, just days after a general election had been called in Britain, the Labour Party held its annual conference, and the night before he was to address the conference, the party leader, Neil Kinnock, wrote a speech outlining the central issues of the coming campaign:

> It was okay, it was a speech about what divided the parties essentially, and what divided the parties was our concept of liberty, freedom, how you get it, what it's for. And I went through a series of illustrations about how people were enfranchised in the Britain of the 1980s but didn't feel any freedom because they had a vote, but if they didn't have a job, they had a vote but if they didn't have good housing, they had a vote but if they were disabled, they had a vote, but if they were old. There were qualifications on the freedom.[2]

Delivering the speech the following day, though, Kinnock realized that he was not reaching his audience as emphatically as he had hoped. He abandoned his notes and began to speak extemporaneously and movingly:

> Why am I the first Kinnock in a thousand generations to be able to get to university? Why is Glenys the first woman in her family in a thousand generations to be able to get to university? Was it because all our predecessors were thick? Did they lack talent,

those people who could sing and play and recite and write poetry? Those people who could make wonderful, beautiful things with their hands? Those people who could dream dreams, see visions? So why didn't they get it? Was it because they were weak, those people who could work eight hours underground and then come up and play football, weak? Those women who could survive eleven childbearings? Were they weak? Does anybody really think that they didn't get what we had because they didn't have the talent or the strength or the endurance or the commitment? Of course not. It was because there was no platform upon which they could stand.[3]

The crowd's enthusiastic response convinced Kinnock that he had not only scored a hit with the party faithful, but that he had formulated his ideas in a way that could reach a wider public. When he stopped speaking, he recollected, '. . . suddenly the place exploded, and I turned around and there were two special branch detectives . . . who had only been with me for three days, and one of them had tears running down his face. So I thought, "Right, I've got it right here"'. The 'thousand generations' speech was later incorporated into a party election broadcast made by *Chariots of Fire* director Hugh Hudson, an advertisement the *New York Times* called 'the single most effective broadcast of the general election contest by any party' (Raines, 1987, p. A3), although it was pointed to during the campaign as evidence of a trend towards glossy 'American-style' political campaigning.

Meanwhile, across the Atlantic, attention was beginning to turn to the Democratic Party's choice of a candidate to face the Republican incumbent, Ronald Reagan, in the presidential elections in November 1988. On 9 June 1987—the day after the Labour broadcast was first aired—Senator Joseph Biden announced his candidacy for the nomination (Dionne, 1987a; Raines, 1987). According to later press accounts, a friend of Senator Biden's saw the Labour Party broadcast while in England and was so impressed with it that he brought back a tape of it for the candidate (Dowd, 1987). Biden identified so strongly with the message in the 'thousand generations' speech that he began incorporating it into his own stump speeches, generally attributing it to Kinnock[4]. However, when he spoke before a large audience in Iowa on 23 August, the attribution was omitted (Dowd, 1987). Portions of that appearance were widely televised, and by mid-September the attention of the press had been drawn to the similarities between Biden's and Kinnock's speech, and Biden was being asked to account for them. Later it was learned that an official in the campaign of Michael Dukakis, a Biden rival for the nomination, had prepared and leaked to the press a tape highlighting the similarities between the two speeches.

The response of the Biden campaign was to defend the use of Kinnock's message as basically fair; the lack of attribution was a minor lapse. An official in the campaign was quoted as saying 'to the degree it wasn't attributed, it was an oversight or inadvertent. . . . The Kinnock message . . . struck him as consistent with his political message his whole political career' (Dowd, 1987).

The considerable public attention which the case attracted illustrates some of the complexities of determining when plagiarism has happened and how seriously it should be regarded. A variety of contextual factors were brought up in such a way as to suggest they were either mitigating or aggravating circumstances. For example, the initial *New York Times* article which broke the story reported that Biden had indeed cited Kinnock on earlier occasions, supporting the interpretation that the lack of attribution on one occasion had simply been a lapse. But the same article suggested that the very fact that the citation was omitted when the speech had been received very successfully, and that Biden did not credit Kinnock in later interviews about that success of the speech, reflected something less than candour.

Factual authenticity became an issue. The *Times* pointed out that the game Kinnock meant by 'football' was not the same game Biden's relatives would have called by that name. A Biden aide was unable to say, when asked, which of the Senator's relatives had been coal miners, but said that since Biden had grown up in a coal mining area he was familiar with the kind of life miners led, implying that Biden had stuck to the truth in spirit, if not in literal detail. The most important element of the story, Biden argued, was true: he supported the sort of equality of opportunity he and Kinnock had spoken of.

Biden's reputation for documenting his sources, and then more generally for accuracy and honesty, was called into question. It was reported, for example, that he had plagiarized in law school

(Dionne, 1987a). Biden admitted to having made an error by not using quotation marks for language from a source, but pointed out that he had named the source in a footnote (Dionne, 1987c). Faculty at his law school agreed that the sort of source misuse found in his work was common among first-year students (Meislin, 1987) and that they did not consider it to be a sign of moral failing. Biden, increasingly on the defensive, was asked to account for factual errors in statements about his background, such as his claim that he had a full scholarship to law school, while in fact he had had a partial scholarship supplemented by need-based financial aid (Biden's response was that he had not seen the distinction as important). His claim to have won an international mock trial competition was viewed sceptically; a journalist reported, somewhat grudgingly, that the competition had been held in Canada and Biden had had a partner, thus suggesting that while literally true, the claim was an exaggeration (Dionne, 1987d).

Biden was also charged with having borrowed from other politicians without (adequate) attribution, a charge which he attempted to deflect by arguing that it was a way of paying homage to those he admired. He attracted support from a number of political commentators who argued that in sampling the rhetoric of a fellow politician, Biden was merely following a well-established tradition (e.g. May, 1987; Teitell, 1987). Columnist William Safire (1987) recounted having experienced a twinge of guilt after modelling part of a speech he wrote for Richard Nixon on one given by Franklin Delano Roosevelt. Confessing his appropriation to one of the writers of the Roosevelt speech, he learned that it too had an antecedent in a political speech of the nineteenth century. The common but unacknowledged presence of the ghostwriter in political discourse, it was noted, creates a large grey area in questions of attribution. The influences on another candidate's speeches were the object of this commentary:

> Like almost all the Democrats in the 1988 campaign, Mr. Gephardt is sounding themes and using words that sound an awful lot like those of the Kennedys. In Mr. Gephardt's case, some of these echoes come from his speechwriter, Robert Shrum, who wrote some of Senator Edward M. Kennedy's most powerful speeches. Thus the question: Where does Mr. Gephardt end and Mr. Shrum

begin? For that matter, where did John F. Kennedy end and Theodore Sorensen, his well-known speechwriter, begin?

Mr. Sorensen said last week that he has become the unwitting ghost writer for candidates he doesn't even support: "I've been reading speeches by candidates for years which borrowed material that I had previously written. President Reagan does it all the time."

(Dionne, 1987e)

Paradoxically, Biden's troubles may be at least partially attributable to the fact that the speech at the centre of the controversy apparently did not involve a speechwriter. Had his speeches been composed by someone whose time was dedicated to that task, attribution might not have been neglected. One Washington speechwriter felt that the outcome of the attention Biden received might be that politicians would give their speechwriters more control over their output (May, 1987), resulting, ironically, in a situation in which concerns about plagiarism would be resolved by politicians using *less* language original to them.

Many of the press accounts have a no-smoke-without-fire tone. Neglecting to attribute Kinnock may have been an oversight, as might the omission of quotation marks on a piece of writing in law school, and Biden may have had legitimate reasons for considering a full financial aid package as equivalent to a full scholarship, and calling a competition in Canada 'international' is technically true, but while the benefit of the doubt might apply to any of these points, it would not comfortably stretch to cover all of them. At the same time, the need to bring in other questionable episodes from Biden's past illustrates that even for those who were least inclined to excuse the use of the Kinnock speech, that alone was not a clear-cut episode of plagiarism. The extent of the wrong depended heavily on whether it was a mistake or intentional deception. Evidence for the latter was lacking in the speech itself, and had to be sought in Biden's past.

Interestingly, one element often given as a reason why plagiarism is wrong was missing from the debate entirely: the harm done to the 'victim' whose words are appropriated. Asked if he felt any sense of loss or damage by the use of his words, without attribution on at least one instance, Neil Kinnock replied 'the opposite is the case. If I am *really* honest I can confess to a little spasm of pleasure'.

By late September, Biden was growing frustrated with the continued scrutiny, which was interfering with his work in the Senate. Eventually it became clear that even if he stayed in the race for the Democratic nomination he would be seriously handicapped, and on 23 September, Biden withdrew from the primary campaign (Dionne, 1987b). Then, in an ironic twist, it was revealed that it had been the Dukakis camp to publicize Biden's use of Kinnock's speech, and the Dukakis campaign director was forced to resign. Criticism now began to centre on the media, who in retrospect were thought to have had too much influence in a primary campaign which featured other allegations of scandal (e.g. Rheem, 1987). So, interestingly, the speech that became prominent in Britain amid criticism that the media were playing too great a role in the election, toppled a US candidate, culminating in the same criticism.

It is noteworthy that the allegation of plagiarism was strong enough to end the candidacy of a strong presidential contender, in spite of mitigating factors, such as the possibility that the lack of attribution had merely been a lapse, and the strong precedents for intertextuality in political speeches. The episode evoked a response which is not uncommon when allegations of plagiarism arise in academic contexts: that plagiarism is so heinous a crime that there can be no mitigation. At the time of the controversy, a former president of Yale University wrote to the *New York Times,*

> The theft of another's intellectual property has always been understood as similar to stealing another's child. It is not a trivial occurrence, excusable on the ground that everyone does it. Only those intent on ensnaring by deception do it.
>
> (Giamatti, 1987, p. 22)

while a law professor called attempts to excuse Biden's plagiarism in law school 'shocking' and 'scandalous' (Damich, 1987, p. 22). A Princeton University lecturer commented that 'To take a piece of writing without acknowledging the creator is plain theft. It is not a trivial matter, not in the classroom, and certainly not in a public forum' (Ragen, 1987, p. A39).

In perspective, this moral outrage is hard to explain. Judges can accept arguments of mitigation in a case of vehicular homicide; can plagiarism actually be worse? Can it be impossible to excuse as a lapse? Cannot some unattributed repetition of language even be accepted as normal practice in some cases? Two of the journalists who covered this story for the *New York Times* might be likely to answer that last question with a decided 'yes'. On 16 September, the byline of Maureen Dowd appeared on a piece containing the following:

> But <u>this week politicians</u> of <u>both parties, some of them partisans of other candidates in the Democratic Presidential race,</u> have pointed out to <u>the press additional instances in which</u> the Delaware Senator <u>has</u> borrowed memorable passages from <u>others'</u> speeches without attributing them.
>
> (p. A1)

The following day E. J. Dionne got the byline for the article in which this appeared:

> <u>This week politicians</u> from <u>both parties—some of them partisans of other candidates in the Democratic Presidential race</u>—told members of <u>the press</u> of <u>additional instances in which</u> Mr. Biden <u>had</u> used the language and syntax of <u>others</u>, including John F. and Robert F. Kennedy and Hubert H. Humphrey.
>
> (p. A1)

(Here and in other examples, words which appear in both texts are underlined.)

Surely that repetition is as clear and as unattributed as Biden's was. That is not to suggest that it was wrong; given that the two writers were collaborating on the same project (reporting the story), recycling a bit of necessary background to that day's story seems only reasonable. However, the same point could be made with equal justice about Joseph Biden and Neil Kinnock, two politicians attempting to end the long reigns of the popular, far-right leaders of their respective countries.

Ultimately, then, what ruined Biden's prospects was not evidence that he had committed deceptive plagiarism in a way that his discourse community would consider inappropriate; the mere accusation was his undoing.

Plagiarism, Civil Rights and a Sense of Proportion

The power of an accusation of plagiarism is such that it did damage to the posthumous reputation of one of the iconic figures of the twentieth century, Martin Luther King, Jr. King's work as a civil rights activist not only contributed to the sweeping changes to US society wrought by the civil rights movement, but also won him the Nobel Peace Prize. Thus considerable shock resulted when it was discovered that King had woven the language of other texts into his student writing, including his doctoral dissertation, without adequate attribution[5]. Researchers at Stanford and Emory Universities working on King's papers found 'passages that are similar or identical to texts King consulted and that he did not adequately cite those source texts' (Martin Luther King, Jr., Papers Project, 1991, p. 23). An extensive comparison of King's student writing with its sources revealed long chunks of language from sources, with no changes or minimal changes; some attribution to these sources, but in a form that a reader would assume to indicate paraphrase, rather than quotation; and analysis reported from secondary sources but with a citation only to the primary source.

As with Joseph Biden, contextual evidence was used to help evaluate the textual plagiarism. There was evidence that King had received some instruction in appropriate forms of citation in academic writing, suggesting that he ought to have understood the implications of his writing strategies, but also that in class discussions he demonstrated a command of the concepts he took up in his writing, indicating that dependence on the language of sources did not disguise an inadequate grasp on the subject matter. The Papers Project found that 'his academic papers, including the dissertation, contain numerous passages that meet a strict definition of plagiarism—that is, *any* unacknowledged appropriation of words or ideas' but that it was too soon to know 'whether King deliberately violated the standards that applied to him as a student. . . . Understanding the reasons for or the significance of King's pattern of textual appropriations will require careful examination of King's student years within a broader biographical and historical context' (Martin Luther King, Jr., Papers Project, 1991, p. 31; italics original).

For some, the evidence of textual plagiarism suggested a clear conclusion: 'unfortunately, there cannot be the slightest doubt that in his student days King became a confirmed plagiarist' (Higham, 1991, p. 106). Even those who believed that the textual plagiarism was evidence merely of clay feet, with King's accomplishments outshadowing his flaws, still maintained that his source use represented a serious ethical breech: 'nothing can be gained by attempting to minimize or understate either the amount of King's plagiarism or the seriousness of the academic wrongdoing that it represented' (Garrow, 1991, p. 86).

Yet an alternative interpretation of King's textual plagiarism exists. This interpretation situates King's student writing, not in the university, but in the discourse community in which he spent most of his life: the African American church. King was the son and grandson of ministers, and after receiving his doctorate in divinity, assumed the position of co-pastor with his father of an Alabama church. Nor was his political activity a departure from his role as pastor: King's opposition to racism was grounded in his belief that it was deeply repugnant to God. As a minister, he felt called to oppose racism. In this sense, his role as a leader in the civil rights movement can be seen as an extension of his ministry, and his textual production, including his speeches, as akin to sermons, and specifically the sermons of what King scholar Keith Miller (1991) terms the African American folk pulpit.

Two features of this rhetorical tradition are memorization and repetition. Illiteracy, enforced by law in the pre-Civil War days and by poverty from the Reconstruction on, meant that African Americans could only preserve and diffuse texts by memorizing them. Miller identifies two sermons which King would have heard as a child, which date back at least to the Civil War decade, and which, he says, are still in current use in the southern United States (1991). Woven together from familiar forms of expression from a wealth of sources, the sermon became a rich intertextual fabric, and 'like generations of folk preachers before him, King often borrowed, modified, and synthesized themes, analogies, metaphors, quotations, illustrations, arrangements and forms of argument used by other preachers' (Miller, 1991, p. 121). King's facility with this technique and his intimate knowledge of canonical texts account for much of his skill as an orator. One biographer attributes King's success on the night in 1955 when he addressed the Montgomery bus boycotters to precisely those factors:

> Playing with the old adage, I suggest that in such cases, 'chance favors the prepared tongue'. While King had not found himself in such a situation before, he was deeply steeped in the Bible, other religious texts, and important American documents. He had heard hundreds, if not thousands, of sermons before, and he had assimilated their themes and rhythms.
> (Gardner, 1995, p. 206)

This background enhanced King's ability to speak without a prepared address. As with Neil Kinnock, one of King's rhetorical peaks came when he was speaking extemporaneously. Addressing the marchers who had converged on Washington in 1963, King's words were 'well received from the opening lines. . . . but only toward the end of the formal remarks did he begin to deviate from the script and hit his stride. Finding his voice . . . King told the world, "I have a dream"' (Gardner, 1995, p. 215).

In addition to supplying the speaker with a vocabulary of ideas and images, memorization and repetition in the rhetoric of the African American pulpit served other functions. They permitted the congregation to participate without the benefit of prayer books and hymnals by being able to predict the coming text, and join in, or respond (Miller, 1990). Such response can be found in the transcription of King's speech to the March on Washington, where the audience frequently affirms King's observations with interjections such as 'My Lord'. The internal repetition of phrases gives the address balance and rhythm, and adds precisely the element of predictability that allows listening to become an active role. In accepting the Nobel Peace Prize in 1964, the repetition of 'I am mindful' creates a steady cadence and a structure for the address:

> *I am mindful* that only yesterday in Birmingham, Alabama, our children, crying out for brotherhood, were answered with fire hoses, snarling dogs, and even death. *I am mindful* that only yesterday in Philadelphia, Missouri, young people seeking to secure the right to vote were brutalized and murdered. *I am mindful* that debilitating and grinding poverty afflicts my people and chains them to the lowest rung of the economic ladder.
>
> (This and other quotations from King's speeches come from the website of the Martin Luther King, Jr., Papers Project at Stanford University)

The repetition extends to texts familiar to the listener, evoking shared knowledge about those texts. Thus in the Nobel Prize speech, King concludes a lengthy credo with references to scripture and to a song with its roots in gospel music and the spiritual: 'and the lion and the lamb shall lie down together and every man shall sit under his own vine and fig tree, and none shall be afraid. I still believe that we shall overcome'. The final language from an old spiritual goes beyond conveying the explicit message of faith in an eventual triumph and evokes images of the suffering and struggles addressed by the fight. Similarly, King's address in Washington began, 'Fivescore years ago, a great American, in whose symbolic shadow we stand today, signed the Emancipation Proclamation'. By reprising the 'great American's' words at Gettysburg ('four score and seven years ago . . .') King reminds the listener of Lincoln's other remarks on the same occasion: that America was 'a nation conceived in liberty and dedicated to the proposition that all men are created equal'. King's reminder was timely, for he went on to tell his listeners—as had Lincoln—that the conception and dedication of the United States in those terms were expressions of intention, of a promise to be fulfilled. King announced 'in a sense we've come to our nation's capital to cash a check'.

But these intertextual threads do more than evoke a context; Miller (1991) has observed that they merge King's voice with its predecessors, and in the process confer the predecessors' authority upon him. 'In such a context the rhetorical issue is always authority, not originality; appropriateness, not personal expression; the Gospel of Jesus Christ, not the views of an individual speaker' (Miller, 1990, p. 78).

King's gift was to tap into the authority that would allow him to lead his flock towards the promised land of equality, to find the appropriate form of inspiring them with his deep conviction that God abominated racism. King used his words, as great orators always have, not merely to share his dream but to make his followers see it as clearly as he did, believe in it as strongly as he did, and fight for it as ardently as he did. Explicitly naming Abraham Lincoln, the Bible or a traditional spiritual in this context was unnecessary, first because his source documents were recognizable to his audience, and secondly, because his overriding purpose was not documentation but inspiration; what mattered was not whether his words were original to him, but what he accomplished with them. This, then, was the rhetorical genre King knew. It should hardly be surprising that when King entered a new discourse community, that of the university, he applied familiar strategies to new rhetorical tasks.

Miller, however, is more interested in the findings of King's textual plagiarism for their ability to invalidate a widespread assumption about King: that his 'intellectual development, ideas, and oratory grew from his philosophical and theological studies in graduate school' (1991, p. 120). Miller argues that King's refusal to observe citation standards demonstrates that it was not his academic experiences which shaped his later performance as an actor and speaker, but that his academic writing was shaped by the discourse of the pulpit.

Writing from a multicultural perspective which she identifies, after W. E. B. Du Bois, as 'the three and fourness of things as an African-American woman, mother, scholar, artist', Bernice Johnson Reagon sees King's writing strategies in a context she understands (1991, p. 112). Reagon points out that the challenge faced by African Americans who succeed in establishing themselves in the dominant culture is to develop an integrated multicultural identity, something she is at pains to distinguish from a dual identity. 'For those of us who straddle', she writes, 'it is necessary to know what is valued both by the African-American tradition and by Western academia' (1991, pp. 118–119). King's roots in the African American church taught him to prioritize finding an authentic voice in the form of expression; the academic world, on the other hand, privileges original content. King, she suggests, was original in a meaningful sense, and in a way which 'straddled' the expectations of the two discourse communities. While King wrote the works in question when he was a member of the university community, he did not write them *as* a member of the university community. He wrote them as the descendent of ministers, as the future minister he was. This also became the context in which King's source use has been interpreted; that is, his textual plagiarism became headline news not because a university student contravened prevailing standards for academic writing, but because the future leader of the US civil rights movement did so.

This points to the first of two notable features of King's plagiarism: its breathtaking irrelevance. Although King's perspective on the civil rights struggle was informed by his readings in philosophy, and although it could be argued that part of what helped him attain the leadership position he came to hold was the respectability of the title 'doctor', the relatively brief period of King's life spent on academic tasks pales to insignificance next to his more important later role. Garrow, quoted above, cautioned against downplaying the 'seriousness of the academic wrongdoing that [King's plagiarism] represented' (1991, p. 86). But it is difficult to specify the sense in which King's plagiarism is at all serious, compared, for example, to the fact that African Americans can now use public toilets and drinking fountains, or the fact that King's work is unfinished, and that while there is no more legal segregation in the United States, there is abundant *de facto* segregation.

The second important feature of this matter, though, is how potentially serious the consequences might have been. The penalties for students who plagiarize can be severe and can include suspension and expulsion. What would have happened to the civil rights movement if King's plagiarism had been discovered while he was a student and he had not been allowed to finish his degree, or had finished under a cloud? Allegations of plagiarism have the power to topple prominent individuals from positions of power, as Joseph Biden learned to his detriment. In an examination of the lengthy investigation the US Federal Bureau of Investigation (FBI) conducted into Martin Luther

King, Jr's life, McKnight reaches the 'appalling conclusion that this Nobelist and one of the most recognized, respected, and honored Americans of the twentieth century was at the time of his death probably the most harassed, hounded, and investigated citizen in the history of the Republic' (1998, p. 6). Although McKnight concludes that the FBI was not aware of King's plagiarism, he speculates about what would have happened had they discovered it. It 'was a mistake that could have ruined King and seriously impaired the black freedom struggle'. Discovering the plagiarism, 'almost certainly the bureau would have gone public with a relentless and hard-hitting campaign. . . . it is hard to see how King could have continued as an effective public figure' (1998, pp. 6–7).

From the Biden and King cases emerge three themes which tend to recur when a case of plagiarism is examined. First, plagiarism is a fuzzy concept. Both the experienced politicians and the commentators on political life who addressed the Joseph Biden case were unable to reach a consensus as to whether he had violated the standards of the genre, while the Project studying King's writing was unable to call his work plagiarism without qualification. Secondly, even where there is agreement that the use of source language has been inappropriate, a variety of explanations are offered: the stress of a campaign, inadvertent omission of a reference, or a cultural background which prizes intertextuality. This highlights the fact that it is difficult to assess an instance of plagiarism without taking the context into account. Finally, even when the allegation is subject to doubt, the mere suggestion of plagiarism can result in extremely weighty consequences. This combination of lack of precision in identifying the act and heavy-handedness in punishing it makes plagiarism a volatile construct.

The purpose of this chapter has been to highlight how context-sensitive plagiarism is. Plagiarism is the product of a particular socio-historical context, and when suspected instances of plagiarism arise, they are evaluated with regard to their background, and not only the textual details. If the writers come from outside the Anglophone academic discourse community, their cultural values are suspected of playing a role. When a specific case is under consideration, the writer's history becomes a factor. In the coming chapters, textual plagiarism in student writing will be examined. In attempting to understand how it should be regarded, and what sort of response is appropriate, the writer's background and the writing context will be seen to be key factors.

Notes

1 These ideas can be found, in various constellations, in works such as Cammish (1997), Deckert (1993), Dryden (1999), Sapp (2002), Sowden (2005a) and Todd (1997). Buranen (1999) relates having heard some of these ideas as commonly circulated explanations for international student plagiarism, and Barks and Watts (2001) and Bloch (2001) give nuanced reviews of some of these points. Ha (2006) believes that common knowledge may be a problematic issue for Vietnamese students, while otherwise casting doubt on many of the ideas in this list.
2 Here and elsewhere, Neil Kinnock's account comes from an interview I conducted with him on 21 June 1999.
3 Transcribed from footage of a Party Election Broadcast from the 1987 campaign at http://news.bbc.co.uk/hi/english/static/vote2001/in_depth/election_battles/1987qt_labour_peb.stm
4 Joseph Biden did not respond to a request for an interview, so this portion of the story is taken from press accounts from the period, as well as Neil Kinnock's report of what Biden later told him.
5 Howard (1999, pp. 120–126, provides an analysis of King's inter-textuality).

3

Learning to write from sources

The view of plagiarism as a dishonest act (as seen, for example, in the common metaphor of plagiarism as theft) masks the difficulty of avoiding plagiarism for academic writers. Theft can be avoided by abstaining from a proscribed act: if you want to avoid stealing someone's property, just leave it where it is. However, since virtually all academic genres, from term paper to thesis to research article, refer to other sources, writers who are concerned about plagiarism cannot simply avoid using other people's texts. Avoiding plagiarism entails knowing how to use sources appropriately. This chapter explores (1) what novice academic writers need to know about plagiarism; (2) what they need to know about source use and (3) how they can learn it.

What Do Writers Need to Know about Plagiarism?

First, students need to know how very seriously plagiarism is regarded in the academic community, and how heavily it is penalized. The tone of violent disapproval that the act evokes was discussed in Chapter 1, and the penalties for it are correspondingly harsh. A study of university plagiarism policies in Britain, the United States and

Australia (Pecorari, 2001) found provisions for punishing plagiarists by lowering their grades, possibly to zero, either on the plagiarized work or in the class for which it was done, by suspending or expelling them from the university, or by denying or revoking degrees (see Baty, 2004, for a case in which a degree was denied for plagiarism and Wasley, 2007, for the revocation of a degree which had been awarded some years earlier). Interestingly, only six universities in the study reported having consequences of a pedagogical nature, such as attending the writing centre.

Students who know that plagiarism can attract 'the academic death penalty' (Howard, 1995), will naturally want to understand what, specifically, the act entails, so that they can avoid it. Here, however, they will encounter difficulty. Although the survey of plagiarism policies mentioned above found that universities are in close agreement as to how to define the act, they give little indication of how the definitions should be applied, and provide no template which a teacher or disciplinary board could use to determine whether a specific text meets the definition. It seems that plagiarism in this respect is like art or pornography: we don't know what it is, but we know it when we see it[1]. An additional, pragmatic definition of plagiarism can therefore be added to the ones presented in Chapter 1: plagiarism is what a person in authority says it is. For a student who wishes to protect an academic career, this definition is possibly the most relevant. However, it does not provide an answer to how a general definition of plagiarism can be applied to a given textual product.

Answering this question is not within the scope of this book, and indeed one of the aims of this book is to demonstrate why an answer is so difficult, if not impossible, to come by. This is because any serious attempt to establish practical benchmarks for plagiarism would have to be based on consensus in the academic community, but that is in short supply. In a study of university lecturers, Roig (2001) found them in disagreement as to which sample texts constituted plagiarism and which appropriate paraphrasing, and also found that nearly one-third completed a paraphrasing task by repeating strings of words from a source in such a way that the repetition was considered, under the terms of the investigation, to be plagiarism. Roig points out that 'unfortunately, the absence of a general operational definition for paraphrasing leaves plenty of room for disagreement as to when a paraphrase might be considered an instance of plagiarism' (2001, p. 320).

The lack of consensus about what specifically counts as plagiarism is also illustrated by the fact that public cases often become sources of controversy, with vocal disagreements as to whether the act in question deserves to be called plagiarism. One such case arose in the autumn of 2005 when a professor at Stockholm University was accused of plagiarism by a researcher in another field, who pointed to multiple passages in the professor's book which repeated verbatim, or with some minor changes, passages from other authors, without quotation marks (Tralau, 2005a, 2005b). In the ensuing debate in the national press, one of the voices defending the professor was an academic from another prestigious Swedish university who thought that the repeated language could be explained by simple error and was therefore not plagiarism. Further, he argued, for it to constitute plagiarism the professor would have had to appropriate something more substantial than language, for example a theoretical model (Harrison, 2005). A university body decided that there were insufficient grounds for bringing disciplinary charges against the professor. A spokeswoman for the body explained that while she herself would have used quotation marks in a similar case, citation practices vary (Gunnarsson, 2005).

A case at a Hong Kong university involved one medical researcher who accused another of having plagiarized a research instrument. A set of complaints and investigations internal to the university was followed by a drawn-out court battle. Academics who were imported from Australia and the UK to testify disagreed about whether plagiarism had occurred (Swinbanks, 1993). Similarly divisive was a case at a US university when a whistleblower pointed out that a professor's published work contained material repeated verbatim, or sometimes with minor changes, from other sources. Colleagues from within and outside of her own university alternately castigated her ('I am convinced to my core that [she] is dirty', p. A20) and defended her ('I see this as a writing error rather than some big ethics issue', p. A19) (Leatherman, 1999). The university investigation took several years, with one body finding the professor guilty and another reaching the opposite conclusion, resulting in her firing, and then her reinstatement (Leatherman, 1999; Smallwood, 2002). Cases like these illustrate a difficulty for teachers, students, disciplinary bodies, and indeed anyone who needs or wants to know on what grounds a text can be labelled as plagiarism: a seemingly clear definition such as the one from the *Concise Oxford Dictionary* presented in Chapter 1, to 'take (the work or an idea of someone else) and pass it off as one's own', proves unexpectedly difficult to apply. Does the 'work or idea' have to be something as substantial as a theoretical model or are a few sentences enough? If the latter, how many? If the alleged plagiarism was a 'writing error', does it mean that the writer was *not* trying to pass someone else's work off as her own? Although individual academics may have a strong internal compass indicating what is and is not acceptable practice in their view, there is little consensus across the academy. What students need to know about plagiarism therefore is that it is a prohibited act and carries stiff consequences, but that individual readers may judge specific texts differently. To avoid plagiarism and to be safe from accusations of it, students need to know how to use sources in a way which is not only acceptable to *some* readers but also unlikely to attract criticism from *any* reader.

What Do Writers Need to Know about Using Sources?

A sizable body of research has investigated source use and citation from several rather varied perspectives. The earliest studies came from the areas of information science and the sociology of science. The findings from these bodies of work fall broadly under two headings. First, considerable effort has been expended on establishing patterns in citation. Statistics on co-citation—the tendency for two or more works on the same topic to be cited together—have been used to identify emerging or important research topics within a field and document how advances in research occur (Price, 1965; Small, 1974, 1977, 2003). Patterns have also been identified for the rate at which individual works enter the literature and then attract increasing or decreasing numbers of citations (Burton and Kebler, 1960; Price, 1965, Shibata et al., 2007).

Similarly, it has been shown that the ideas for which a given work will be cited are to some extent predictable. Frequently cited papers are likely to be cited for a single proposition (Small, 1978), although when articles are noticed and cited by more than one research community, the frequently mentioned proposition may be different in each community (Cozzens, 1982). Whether a paper becomes prominent in a given research area may also determine whether citations to it refer mainly to a single proposition or to a range of ideas presented in the paper (Cozzens, 1985); in the former case, it may be more likely that the paper will be cited negatively as well as positively (Allen, 1997).

A second area of investigation has been citer motivation; that is, how do writers choose what to cite and when? (The useful distinction made by Thompson and Ye, 1991, between the *writer* of a new text and the *author* of an earlier one cited in the new text, is adopted here.) A range of disparate—and sometimes contradictory—motivations have been put forward. These include compensating the cited author, as a 'reaffirmation of the underlying general norms of scientific behavior' (Kaplan, 1965, p. 181), and as an act of persuasion (Gilbert, 1977). Becher's informants identified a number of factors influencing citation behaviour, including laying a foundation for the ideas put forward in the new work. Citation is used 'to suggest that you are keeping good intellectual company' and 'serves a social and institutional as much as an epistemological function' (Becher and Trowler, 2001, p. 114). Another survey, though, found that social or instrumental motivations were *not* important in the decision to cite (Shadish et al., 1995). Self-citation, according to Hyland, is a 'significant means of promoting a scholarly reputation' (2003, p. 259). In other words, the decision to cite can be made with an eye to what is good for research, or what is good for the researcher. (For a thorough discussion of citer motivation studies, see White, 2004.)

The research on citation coming from the sociology of science and information science traditions has aimed to answer questions about citation within the community of researchers: how does the focus of scientific inquiry change over time? (e.g. Small, 1977); how can important research be distinguished from the more mundane? (e.g. Gilbert, 1977; Moravcsik and Murugesan, 1975); how can researchers tell which of the citations they find indexed are most relevant? (Lipetz, 1965); what can we learn about the ways of scholarly communities from how they cite? (e.g. Becher and Trowler, 2001; Small, 2003). However, despite the rather detailed findings that had been amassed by the 1980s, there was still a 'need for a theory of citing' (Cronin, 1981) and in consequence a need for new methods:

> To understand why an author cites in a particular way at a particular time we would need, to put it crudely, to step inside the author's head. . . . Consequently, direct questioning would appear to be the most sensible method of trying to penetrate this private world.
>
> (p. 21)

The shift in the focus of research interest towards the reasons for writers' choices made citation studies an area of interest for linguists, as noted by Swales (1986) in an influential paper which put citation onto the linguistics research agenda. Swales also observed that although bibliometricians and sociologists of science could benefit from a linguistic perspective on citation research, linguistics had had no significant influence on or from either area. Since then a considerable body of research into citation from a linguistic perspective has arisen (although White, 2004, notes that there is still relatively little cross-pollination on the topic among linguistics, bibliometrics and sociology of science).

A few studies have taken the direct approach that Cronin called for, interviewing writers or disciplinary insiders about citation (e.g. Dong, 1996; Harwood, 2008; Hyland, 1999). Another approach has been somewhat less direct, mapping the effects of citation on a text. One of the most influential of these is Swales' CARS (create a research space) model (1981, 1990, 2004). The CARS model describes a series of 'moves' and 'steps' that writers of research articles perform in their introductions, in order to set the context for their own research, which is presented in later sections. The first move is 'establishing a territory', which is accomplished with the help of citations to existing work within that territory. Citations may also play a role in the second move, 'establishing a niche', in which the writer identifies the need for additional research in the territory, for example by establishing that there is a gap in the existing knowledge, thus paving the way for the third move in which the writer presents the topic of the article.

By showing how the state of current research on a topic can be used to justify an addition to it, the CARS model highlights the connections between the act of citation and the objectives of the text. The same message emerges from Berkenkotter and Huckin's (1995) study of the progress of a research article through the publication process. Among the changes the writer made to accommodate referees' comments was the addition of a number of references. The writer was ultimately somewhat uncomfortable with this addition, saying she felt it amounted to telling a 'phony story' (p. 55) since the new references created a context for her research which was not the one from which it originally sprang. To her readers, however, that broadened context was 'in a sense, the *real* story' (p. 59, italics in the original); references to the right sources added value to the article and made the findings more meaningful. An aspect of citation, therefore, of which novice writers need to be aware, is the important role it plays in advancing the purposes of the citing text.

Writers also need to be conscious of the many formal options for incorporating citations into a text (Thompson and Tribble, 2001), some of which are illustrated in Figure 3.1.

Citations can appear in 'integral' or 'non-integral' forms (Swales, 1990). An integral citation is one in which the name of the source author appears as a syntactic element in the citing sentence, as in example (a) in Figure 3.1, while non-integral citations are outside the structure of the citing sentence, as in example (b). In addition, some researchers identify a more general class of reference called 'summary' (Jacoby, 1987), 'general references' (Salager-Meyer, 1999) or 'non-citational' references (Tadros, 1993) in which mention is made of a school of thought, trend, prominent researcher, etc., rather than to a specific research work (c). Either integral or non-integral citations can be coupled to material reported in two ways, quotation, or paraphrase[2].

Citation formats include in-text references, in which the author is named somewhere in the running text (e.g., a, b); footnotes or

> a. According to Brie (1995), the moon is made of cheese.
> b. The moon is very likely to consist of cheese (Brie, 1995).
> c. Dairy researchers have made considerable recent progress in ascertaining the composition of the moon.
> d. Brie claims that the moon is almost certainly made of cheese (1995, p. 25).
> e. There is a growing consensus that the moon is likely to be made of cheese[15].
> f. The moon is now thought to be made primarily of cheese [3].
> g. For a review of research into the moon's lactose content, see [3].
> h. Bries (1995) report of the whey content of the moon provided solid evidence for this contention.
> i. The first hard evidence for the moon's caseous composition was provided by Brie (1995).

FIGURE 3.1 *Citation forms (these cheesy examples are adopted in the tradition of Swales, 1990).*

endnotes, in which a numbered reference directs the reader to a correspondingly numbered note at the end of the page, article, chapter, etc. in which the source is named (e); and numbered references within the text, which correspond to a numbered list of references at the end of the text. Such numbered references are more likely to include non-integral citation, as in (f), but may also involve integral citation, as in (g). Citations may be connected to brief, *en passant* mentions of the cited work or a longer discussion of it (Swales, 1986).

Integral citations in particular may contain a reporting verb, such as *claims* in (d) (and Jacoby, 1987, identified reporting *nouns* such as *report* in (h) as well). Reporting verbs are believed to be an important aspect of citation for learners to master, not least of all because there are so many of them—Thompson and Ye (1991) found over 400—and because they convey a range of widely differing meanings, and are revealing of the writer's orientation to, or evaluation of, the reported proposition. As a result, attempts have been made to create a typology for classifying reporting verbs. An early and quite detailed typology is Thompson and Ye's (1991), according to which reporting verbs are classed as *author acts,* relating to what the source author did (*state, discuss*) or *writer acts,* about the writer's processes. Author acts are further subcategorized according to the nature of the process: *textual verbs* (Thompson and Ye's examples include *state, say*), *mental verbs* (*believe, consider*) and *research verbs* (*find, measure*). These groups are further subdivided according to the author's stance towards, or evaluation of, the reported proposition, which can be positive (the author endorses the reported proposition as true, e.g. *accept, point out*), negative (the author represents the reported proposition as wrong, e.g. *attack, question*) or be neutral (*focus on, undertake*).

Writer act verbs include *comparing verbs,* which place one source text in relation to another (*correspond to*), and *theorizing verbs,* which put the source text in relation to the new, citing work (*account for*). The same three stance options are open to the reporting writer, although they are labelled differently. *Factive verbs* suggest that the writer concurs with the reported proposition (*show*); *counter-factive verbs* express the writer's disagreement (*confuse*) and *non-factive verbs* allow the reporting writer to remain neutral (*propose*). Writer act verbs also have the dimension *writer's interpretation,* with four broader subcategories. *Author's discourse interpretation verbs* allow the reporting writer to relate the source author's proposition to the source text (*add, remark*). *Author's behaviour interpretation verbs* put forward the reporting writer's understanding of why the source author expressed a given proposition (*admit, warn*). *Status interpretation verbs* express the writer's understanding of how the reported proposition relates to the new text (*account for, conform to*), and *non-interpretation verbs* allow the reporting writer to portray the reference as objective (*employ, use*).

What may not be immediately apparent from this description is that the categories are permeable, and reporting verbs can occupy more than one of them. What *is* likely to be apparent is the complexity of this taxonomy. This is due to the nature of reporting verbs; they encode a great deal of information on a number of dimensions. Thus, selecting an appropriate reporting verb entails making choices about how to represent the orientation of the writer and the author towards the reported proposition, as well as how the proposition served the original text and how it serves the new one. More fundamentally, making those choices requires critical reading abilities and a clear sense of direction for the new text. As a result, the selection of reporting verbs is by no means straightforward for the novice writer. The task may be made additionally difficult by the fact that the 'flavour' of the reporting verbs may not be entirely transparent. *Acknowledge*, for example, has negative associations; the thing that is acknowledged is either inherently negative (for the speaker) or judged as negative. However, demonstrating that—as opposed to arriving at that conclusion by way of native-speaker intuition—requires an examination of the contexts in which *acknowledge* occurs (Hunston, 1995).

A final reporting verb choice has to do with the form of the verb. Especially common reporting verb forms used in citations are in the present tense (example (d) in Figure 3.1), the past tense (i) and present perfect (c) (Swales and Feak, 2004). Further, the reporting verb may be active (d) or passive (f).

In short, citations can occur in a range of forms. However, and importantly, the forms do not vary freely. Instead, a number of factors in the writing context suggest which form or forms may be most appropriate. One of these is the discipline within which the citing text is produced. Significant differences have been identified in how disciplines use citation. Direct quotation, for example, is quite normal in the 'soft' fields, i.e. the social sciences and humanities (Pickard, 1995, found that one third of the citations in a corpus of linguistics writing were attached to quotations), but it is extremely rare in the 'hard' areas of the natural sciences and engineering (Dubois, 1988; Hyland, 1999; Pecorari, 2006; Salager-Meyer, 1999; Thompson, 2000[3]). Integral citations may also occur less often in hard disciplines than soft (Hyland, 2000; Thompson, 2000) although Charles (2006a) found integral citations slightly more frequent in the hard field included in her corpus, a finding which was perhaps due in part to the reference styles chosen by her writers[4]. Variation is also found in the choice of reporting verb, with hard fields more likely than soft ones to use research verbs, while the reverse is true for textual verbs (Charles, 2006a; Hyland, 2000).

In addition, the genre or type of text is responsible for some variation in citation forms. For example, the dissertations studied in Thompson and Tribble (2001) differed in several respects from research articles (Hyland, 1999). Textbooks appear to use citations less frequently than research articles (Myers, 1992), something which Tadros (1993) suggests may be due to the textbook author's desire to establish his or her authority rather than appeal to someone else's. Variation in citation has even been found within the rhetorical sections of the same work (Hanania and Akhtar, 1985; Thompson and Tribble, 2001).

These differences in the uses that disciplines, genres and even sections of texts make of citations amount to patterns. What is important to note, though, is that the patterns are not arbitrary; in a number of ways, they are closely tied to the rhetorical needs of the reader, the writer and the text. For example, whether an integral or a non-integral citation is used determines in part the message the citation sends. Integral citations are 'author prominent' while non-integral citations are 'information-prominent' (Weissberg and Buker, 1990, pp. 43–45). A non-integral citation such as (1) below draws attention primarily to the fact being reported, while in the integral citation in (2), the fact that Brie is the source for the information is at least equally salient.

1   The moon is very likely to consist of cheese (Brie, 1995).

2   According to Brie (1995), the moon is made of cheese.

Further, the impression given by (1) is that the writer is confident about asserting the fact in question, and the role of the citation is to confirm what the writer already knew, and/or knows to be generally accepted in the field, while in (2) the writer calls heavily upon the authority of the source—in the process, relinquishing some of his or her own. Other factors may come into play to modify this balance. Groom (2000), exploring the interplay of 'propositional responsibility' and 'textual voice', shows that between these two extremes the writer and author can share responsibility for a proposition approximately equally, as in (3), or with the author dominant, but the writer's voice still present, as in (4) (both examples from Groom, 2000, p. 22):

3   As Brie (1999) points out, the moon may be made of cheese.

4   Brie (1999) points out that the moon may be made of cheese.

In both examples, the reporting verb, *points out,* suggests that the writer joins Brie in evaluating the proposition as a true one, and by assuming the position of assessing the worth of Brie's assertion, the writer gains a degree of authority approximately equal to Brie's. The effect in (3) of placing the citation in the adverbial is to leave the possibility open that the writer arrived at the conclusion independently of Brie, thereby establishing symmetrical authority for the two: *Brie and I both know this.* In (4) Brie is in subject position and is given undivided credit for the proposition, but the writer gains a lesser degree of authority by having the perspicacity to realize that Brie is correct.

Looking beyond the citing sentence, the larger context may play a role as well. In isolation, (4) may reduce the prominence of the writer, but the effect is less strong if that sentence appears in a context like (5):

5   Recent years have seen significant breakthroughs in identifying the composition of astral bodies. Brie (1999) points out that the moon may be made of cheese, and a growing body of evidence suggests that much of the Milky Way is aptly named (Gorgonzola, 1996; Wensleydale, 2001).

Verb form can also be linked to the rhetorical purposes of the text. Hanania and Akhtar (1985) found that present tense (for all verbs, not only reporting verbs) was used more in the introductions to science theses than in other sections, and conclude that this 'reflects the tendency in an introduction for the writer to make background generalizations, establish assumptions, and state the purpose of the work' (p. 53). In other words, the present is used in introductions because accomplishing the purpose of an introduction entails describing the existing situation which is the background to the research.

Similarly, Shaw (1992) identified patterns in the form of the reporting verbs which could be linked to the rhetorical demands of the theses they appeared in, and concluded that 'tense and voice are therefore not chosen to indicate function, but in most cases follow naturally from higher-level decisions' (p. 312; the findings of Thompson's 2005 study of citation in theses coincide with this). The novice academic writer needs, therefore, not only to be able to deploy the full range of citation forms, but to distinguish the different rhetorical effects each has and to make appropriate choices depending on the context.

The connection between form and function may be mediated by the demands of the discourse community. Disciplinary differences were prominent in Charles' (2006b) study of citation in theses in two academic areas. Writers in the hard field gave their reporting verbs non-human or dummy *it* subjects, while those in the soft field used more human subjects than the other two categories put together. Further differences were found in the types of structures used with each subject type, leading Charles to conclude that:

> there are fundamental differences in the way that claims are grounded and made persuasive in the two disciplines and this reflects key differences in the nature and construction of knowledge in the two fields.
>
> (2006b, p. 506)

In other words, the form of the reporting clause reflects the conventional expectations of the writer's discipline. The novice writer needs, then, not only to be able to manipulate the range of citation forms to give the desired rhetorical effects, but also to know how those effects will be received by the discourse community, and thus be able to align the form of the citation with its intended purpose.

This chapter began by asking what novice writers need to know to avoid plagiarism. A concise answer to that question can now be seen to be 'rather a lot'. Students need to know not only what plagiarism is but also how to avoid it by using sources appropriately. Good source use entails understanding the role of citation in the life of the disciplinary community and in its texts; mastering the range of forms in which citations can be included in a text; understanding the rhetorical effects that formal choices have on the text, and the purposes for which citations can be used and knowing about the conventional expectations of the discourse community. This full, complex understanding of source use is important; there is evidence that students who use a greater range of citation forms, for a wider range of purposes, have their work assessed more favourably (Petrić, 2007).

How Do They Learn It?

Novice academic writers therefore need to learn to perform a rather complex set of skills in a way that is not only broadly acceptable to the academic community but which also meets the specific demands of their disciplines. How do they do it? Explicit instruction is, of course, one route, although there are limitations on how much it can accomplish. Academic writing courses are widespread and potentially valuable, but not all students have access to them. Where available, they make up only a small part of the curriculum, due to financial and time constraints, including the competition between 'content' and 'ancillary' courses (a contestable division but one which is frequently named in discussions about time allocated to skills like writing). In addition, citation and source use is only one aspect of academic writing, and often receives little attention in textbooks (Thompson and Tribble, 2001) and courses. As Harwood points out, in EAP materials 'the spotlight remains on how citation is used, rather than what it is for' (2004, p. 86). When teachers in a student's discipline attempt to address writing issues, they may focus on lexico-grammatical points and fail to identify higher level rhetorical issues and the ways that differing epistemologies may play out textually (Ballard and Clanchy, 1991). In addition, explicit instruction can only address those points of which teachers are consciously aware. This last may seem an obvious point, but as will be seen below, it is nonetheless a very important one.

Another approach to academic writing—and other closely related tasks, such as defining and investigating relevant research questions—is learning by doing, and metaphors of apprenticeship are often applied to the postgraduate learning experience (Belcher, 1994; Berkenkotter et al., 1988). At least four important elements in apprenticeship can be identified; unfortunately, problems with realizing each of these have been identified in the growing body of research into thesis supervision. First, for the apprenticeship to be successful, the expert—the supervisor, in a thesis-writing context—and the apprentice—the student—must agree on the nature of their task and their respective spheres of responsibility. This, however, may be easier said than done. Disagreement can arise in a number of areas: about specific ways of working, such as what sort of texts the supervisor will read and comment on, as well as about who should make such decisions (Dysthe, 2002); about rhetorical issues, such as how the existing literature should be linked to the student's own research (San Miguel and Nelson, 2007); about the critical distance that needs to be maintained to the literature (Belcher, 1994); or about the extent to which the supervisor should be directive or allow the student autonomy (Krase, 2007).

In order to arrive at agreement—or to overcome disagreement—on issues like these a second necessary ingredient is good communication between the supervisor and student, but this too cannot be taken for granted. Supervisors–student pairs may fail to raise important issues for explicit discussion (Dysthe, 2002) or may experience misunderstanding when they try to communicate (Krase, 2007), or communicate at cross-purposes (Belcher, 1994).

Third, an apprenticeship ideally involves some degree of collaboration (albeit asymmetrical, as Dysthe, 2002, notes). In practice, this does not always occur, or at least not to a degree that is satisfying to both parties. Dong (1998) found that PhD supervisors reported that they gave more help than the students reported receiving, and that students wanted more involvement and cooperation from their supervisors. In an interview-based study of three PhD student–advisor relationships, Belcher (1994) found the most successful was the one in which the advisor was fully engaged in the research in a collaborative and hands-on way.

Hands-on collaboration is one of the key characteristics of the mode of learning that Lave and Wenger (1991) have termed *legitimate peripheral participation* (LPP). LPP involves the learner taking part in activities which are authentically part of the repertoire of an expert practitioner (and thus legitimate) by carrying out tasks which do not require the full range of skills, and which make a smaller contribution to the larger task (and are thus peripheral). A learner who is involved in the activity of the expert is physically situated to be able to observe it, and to learn from observation as well as from hands-on practice. The same physical proximity allows the expert to monitor, and guide, the learner's efforts. This mutual visibility is an important feature of LPP, and when it is removed from the equation, important learning opportunities are lost. In an unsuccessful site of learning described by Lave and Wenger (1991), novices and experts were physically separated by the design of the workplace, and the novices were assigned tasks which could be completed with only minimal instruction and little or no supervision, while the experts performed more demanding tasks out of the sight of the novices. As a result, very little learning took place.

When the infrastructure does not separate experts and learners, the crafts traditionally taught through apprenticeship—butcher, baker, candlestick maker—are well suited to observation, involving, as they do, physical processes. The same cannot be said for writing: under ordinary circumstances neither the composing process nor the writer's cognitive processes which underlie it are directly observable. Academic apprentices can, however, substitute two forms of indirect observation. First, they receive feedback on their writing from supervisors and other experienced members of the discourse community. Secondly, the process of doing and writing about research inevitably entails reading research texts, which serve as models from which students extrapolate the principles of good writing in their fields (Shaw, 1991). Thus, instead of the learner observing the expert's processes and vice versa, each observes the other's written product, and can use it—more or less consciously—to infer something about the processes.

The success of such indirect observations depends on the reliability of the reader's inferences, and making accurate inferences about how sources have been used presents a challenge. Certain aspects can be observed; for example, in (6) below, the year of publication of the sources is identified, and the reference list would (in a real context) identify whether they are books, journal articles, etc. Some evidence is available to show that novice writers note these visible features of citation, and use them to learn about the tendencies in their fields to cite certain kinds of sources (Pecorari, 2006).

6 Although Brie (1990) reported that the moon is made of a smooth, creamy cheese, Stilton attacked his claim as being 'based on too little data, much of which is suspect' (1992, 153).

However, it is not only impossible to observe the processes that led to the presence of citations in the text, inferences about them cannot be confirmed on the basis of the new text alone. For example, it appears in (6) that the proposition from Brie has been paraphrased, while the one from Stilton has been quoted. However, unless the reader has read both sources and has an encyclopaedic memory of them (unlikely) or takes the trouble to obtain them and make a comparison (almost equally unlikely), those are assumptions. The writer may have misquoted Stilton or may in fact be quoting Brie but have forgotten the quotation marks. A reader would also tend to assume that the writer has read both Brie and Stilton and has contrasted their views, but that is just another untested inference; it may be that the writer has read only Stilton and is taking the account of Brie from it.

All of this is invisible to the reader because the *real* relationship between the citing text and the cited text is hidden, or *occluded*[5]. To counter the effect of occlusion, academic texts make use of a meta-language intended to signal how the writer has used sources. It is worth noting that this meta-language constitutes a sort of shorthand, and a rather minimalistic one at that. Two (or four) small marks, quotation marks, convey this idea: *the words which appear between these marks have been taken verbatim from the text which is named here.* Square brackets around part of a quotation assert: *I, the writer, have changed a word or words that appeared in the original, but promise that the change does not affect the interpretation of the content in any substantive way.* An ellipsis, three small dots, tells the reader that *words that appeared in the original have been omitted, but the omission does not distort the meaning in this context.*

Other metatextual signals are entirely absent, and their existence must be inferred from the lack of others. Citations in a text serve to *attribute* the proposition to another source but where attribution is not present, the writer is assumed to *aver* the proposition (Sinclair, 1986, 1987). Thus, in (7) below, Stilton apparently challenges the proposition that the moon is made of cheese but the absence of attribution for that proposition suggests that the writer is averring it, asserting it on the basis of his or her own knowledge and authority. Averral is the default condition; nothing is needed to signal it.

7 Although it is now known that the moon is made of cheese, as recently as the 1980s some skeptics still challenged the idea (e.g. Stilton, 1992).

Similarly, quotation is signalled, most often by the use of quotation marks (or sometimes in a separate block, or by some other typographical or textual device). However, when material attributed to a source is *not* signalled as quotation, the assumption is that the wording is original to the new text and *not* taken from an earlier one. The signal for paraphrase, in other words, is to use no signal at all apart from a citation.

The metatextual signals associated with citation are, therefore, subtle at best. Nonetheless, when the writer uses these signals in the conventional way and the reader is experienced enough to decode them in the way they were intended, they suffice to notify the reader about the role that earlier texts played in the new one. However, success depends on the accurate use of a shared set of conventions, and in the case of inexperienced members of the academic community, the ability to use and interpret the signals fluently cannot be taken for granted.

If the extent of the problem were simply that inexperienced writers may not grasp immediately how things are done, it would be a minor problem indeed. However, to return to the apprenticeship model of learning, the purpose of having novices engage in peripheral but legitimate tasks is to create a situation in which they can note the skilled performance of the expert, and receive feedback on their own less skilled efforts. Occlusion keeps this from happening in two ways. First, if the novice makes the wrong inferences about how experienced writers use sources, there is nothing visible in the experts' texts to reveal the misunderstanding. Secondly, the expert reader is handicapped in judging whether the novice has sent the right signals. If the writer appears to be averring where attribution is called for, or omits quotation marks around language which was taken verbatim from a source, there will ordinarily be nothing in the new text to alert the reader to that fact so the writer's less-than-satisfactory performance will not be noted.

This chapter has argued that to avoid plagiarism, academic writers need to understand the act, which is difficult given the diverse views that established academics have of it. In addition, writers need to be capable of using sources in an effective and appropriate way. The learning curve is a steep one, because citation is a complex aspect of writing. It is also an occluded aspect, which gives reason to think that novice writers learning this central skill may not have all the resources they need to do so. The next chapter will examine the source use of 17 such writers.

Notes

1. This point has also been made by Anderson (1998), and by Stearns (1999), who cites one writer for the parallel between plagiarism and pornography, and another for the need to cite with great care when writing about plagiarism, although I did not come across either of those sources until I had first made this point in print. Stearns' compulsion—and mine—to acknowledge even coincidental similarities between texts illustrates what a powerful taboo plagiarism is.
2. Hyland (2000) uses the term 'summary' for paraphrase, perhaps in recognition of the fact that many references which do not involve direct quotation report larger order ideas, for example the main argument in a text, rather than repeating specific propositions in a re-worded form. While these two are indeed rather distinct ways of reporting the content of a source, both involve the retelling of source content in a formulation determined by the writer, and so *paraphrase* will be used here for both.
3. It should be noted that of the two disciplines in Thompson's (2000) study, one, agricultural botany, falls rather neatly under the 'hard' heading, but the other, agricultural economics, is less obviously a typical 'soft' field.
4. Swales is probably correct in suggesting that the reference format—which is often determined by editorial or institutional policy, rather than by the writer—plays a role in determining to what extent integral citations will be used. Authors' names lend themselves to integral citation more readily than numbers, so an in-text reference style would seem to favour integral citations. However, the existence of integral citations with numbered references demonstrates that Charles (2006a) is right in pointing out that other factors must be involved as well.
5. Swales (1996) described occluded academic genres such as job applications, which are less visible than more public genres such as research articles. I am adapting the idea of occlusion and applying it to a specific textual feature, citation.

4

The texts

The previous chapter outlined the areas of knowledge and skills that novice academic writers need to have, or to acquire. That was the background to an investigation of source use in student writing which aimed to answer the following questions:

1. How effectively do inexperienced academic writers use sources?
2. Does plagiarism or other inappropriate source use occur in their texts?
3. What causes novice writers to integrate sources in their writing the way they do?
4. How do they learn about writing from sources?
5. How do experienced writers react to student source use?

In this chapter a set of texts produced by students will be examined in order to answer the first two questions. The third and fourth questions will be addressed in Chapter 5, and the fourth and fifth in Chapter 6.

Investigating Source Use

This section presents a brief overview of the methods used in this investigation; full details of the methods used for gathering and analysing the data can be found in the Appendix. The investigation consisted of three elements: an analysis of student writing, interviews with some of the writers and interviews with their supervisors. The corpus of student writing was made up from portions of nine master's and eight PhD theses[1] from three universities in Great Britain. The writers were all non-native speakers of English (NNSEs). The sections included in the corpus came in most cases from the early sections of the theses, as they had a relatively high density of citations. A sample with an average length of approximately 3,000 words was taken from each thesis to give a total of just over 51,000 words. The samples from the master's subcorpus were (with two exceptions) early drafts of sections which the writers intended to include in their theses, while the PhD samples came from completed theses. Four academic areas were represented: the humanities, social sciences, engineering and natural sciences. The composition of the corpus is shown in Table 4.1.

The master's students and their supervisors were voluntary participants in what was described as a study of student writing, and were asked to supply recently completed work which was planned for inclusion in the theses. Because the PhD samples came from final drafts, protecting the writers' identities was especially important, so no contact was made with the students, their supervisors or their departments. Samples of their theses were taken from copies held by their university libraries. Students and supervisors are referred to here by pseudonyms, and their departments and universities are not named.

The writing samples were then compared to the sources they cited. A total of 481 sources were used and/or referred to in the student corpus, of which 363, or 75 per cent, could be obtained. Because the sources gathered for comparison were all cited in the writing samples, or in some other way identified by the writers, it is possible that the picture of source use that emerges from the comparison may be incomplete. Specifically, some sources may have been used but not identified by the writer, in which case they were not considered at all in this investigation.

Using the results of the comparison to determine whether the student texts contained textual plagiarism involved deciding whether the three criteria identified in Chapter 1 had been met:

TABLE 4.1 Composition of the corpus by field and level of study.

Writing sample	Master's		PhD	
	Writer	Length (number of words)	Writer	Length (number of words)
Science	Ingrid	2,136	Sci1	2,871
	Erden	1,373	Sci2	2,805
Engineering	Yves	2,240	Eng1	3,261
	Pierre	5,025	Eng2	3,237
Social Science	Graciela	4,227	SS1	2,314
	Maria	3,651	SS2	2,665
Humanities	Roula	2,430	H1	3,439
	Kwan	2,797	H2	3,474
	Helen	3,510		
Total number of words			51,455	
Average number of words per writing sample			3,027	

1 whether there were similarities of language and/or ideas between two texts;

2 whether the similarities came about because one text drew upon another and

3 whether the intertextual relationship (if any) was signalled appropriately.

Each of these points presents its own methodological difficulty. Observing similarities of language is relatively straightforward, but the possibility exists that an idea repeated from a source in a considerably different form escaped detection (particularly in the engineering and science texts). The second criterion has to do with the writing *processes*; however, what was available for observation here (as is usually the case when plagiarism is suspected) is the *product*.

Deciding that a text contains plagiarism, therefore, entailed using the finished product—in this case, specifically its similarities to a source—and concluding that the similarities were so great that coincidence was *not* a viable explanation. This is problematic, however, since no empirically validated baseline figure exists to indicate how much similarity between two texts is likely to occur coincidentally[2]. Without a 'plagiarism threshold', judgements about whether similarities are due to copying or chance are inevitably impressionistic, and will vary from individual to individual. Instead of applying an arbitrary threshold, the approach adopted here is to describe relationships between the student texts and their sources both quantitatively and qualitatively, and to discuss the likelihood that the relationship is coincidental, as well as the likelihood that the relationship might put the student at risk of an accusation of plagiarism.

The third criterion hinges on what is appropriate, and as Chapter 2 established, there is considerable disunity on this point. For the purposes of this analysis, only fully transparent source use is considered to be fully appropriate. The idea of *transparent source use* builds upon the notion of occlusion introduced in Chapter 3. Because the real relationship between a new text and the sources it uses is occluded, the writer has a responsibility to signal it for the reader, by providing references, quotation marks, etc. In particular, three overlapping aspects of source use must be signalled by the writer:

1 identity of the source: does the reader understand which sources materially influenced the new text?

2 content: does the reader receive an accurate impression of what the source text said?

3 language: does the reader understand whether the language comes from the source (i.e. whether the writer has used quotation or paraphrase)?

When a text is written in such a way that an experienced reader makes the correct assumptions about the ways sources have been used, then the source use is transparent.

Adopting the transparency principle does not entirely resolve the problems associated with determining whether the third plagiarism criterion has been met, not least of all because it does not circumvent the problem that specific instances of opaque source use would be labelled plagiarism by some people but not others (e.g. Errey, 2002; Roig, 2001). However, applying the transparency principle transforms the question of interest into one more readily susceptible of an answer, and arguably more relevant to student writers: instead of *did this writer plagiarize?* the question becomes *is this writer safe from accusations of plagiarism?*

Opaque Source Use in the Writing Samples

When source use is not transparent, the result is not always textual plagiarism. Opaque source use is, however, an indication of a problem, and can therefore be a valuable reflection of the writer's skills. In this section, therefore, all three areas of transparency will be examined.

Transparency of Language

One of the aspects of transparent source use most closely linked to plagiarism is language: the reader should understand whether the language used to express an idea has been taken from the source (i.e. quotation). Unless language is enclosed in quotation marks (or the equivalent, as when a longer quotation is set off in narrower margins), a reader is likely to assume that the form of expression is original to the writer. If the assumption later proves to be wrong, an accusation of plagiarism can ensue. To test whether that assumption was justified in the student texts, an initial step in the investigation was to identify language repeated from the sources. The student corpus contained 182 quotations, which, like that in (8), were signalled as such (here and throughout, the source for examples is given in square brackets).

> 8   The definition of the language feature known as metaphor has never been a straightforward matter. Different opinions have been put forward by philosophers, linguists and anthropologists.

'Philosophy, psychology, literary theory and science—all find themselves challenged to define their scope and aims by this presence at the heart of their activities, this one phenomenon, metaphor' (Miall, 1982: xiii).

[Roula]

Quotations were present in each of the nine social studies and humanities texts; in addition, one quotation appeared in one of the master's engineering samples. The relatively common use of quotation in the soft fields and its scarcity in the hard fields reflects common practices in these disciplines, as noted in Chapter 3.

Even more common, though, was the repetition of language from the source without quotation marks (or other equivalent signals), either verbatim, as in (9), or with minor changes, as in (10). Here and throughout, the first in the pair of extracts comes from the student writing sample and the second from the source. Words which appear in both have been underlined.

9a <u>Plant tissue culture storage methodology has been under development for some 15–20 years. During that time, considerable progress has been made, particularly in the cryopreservation of living organism</u>*.

[Erden] *sic*

9b <u>Plant tissue culture storage methodology has been under development for some 15–20 years. During that time, considerable progress has been made, particularly in the cryopreservation of living organisms</u> in general and of plant material in particular (Ashwood-Smith and Farrant, 1980; Kartha, 1985; Grout and Morris, 1987).

[Withers, 1991, p. 245]

10a <u>Sensitivity, S, is usually defined as the ratio</u> between <u>the undisturbed shear strength to the remoulded shear strength</u>, as <u>determined either from vane test or from unconfined compression test</u>.

[Eng2]

10b Sensitivity, *St,* is usually defined as the ratio of the undisturbed shear strength to the remoulded shear strength, determined either from vane tests or from unconfined compression tests.
[Brenner et al., 1981, pp. 214–215]

Where changes were made, they were often the local alterations that Howard (1999, p. xvii) describes as patchwriting: 'copying from a source text and then deleting some words, altering grammatical structures, or plugging in one synonym for another'. Thus in (11), *preferable to* has been replaced with *better than,* and in (12) the adverbial has been moved from the end of the original sentence to the beginning of the new one.

11a On the other hand, Verma and Beard (1981) have emphasized the simplicity of the questionnaire. They suggest that the form of the questions should avoid any suggestion that one kind of answer is better than another.
[SS2]

11b The form of the question should avoid any suggestion that one kind of answer is preferable to another and must not assume facts not in evidence; e.g. to ask which of the following reasons would you give for thinking that teaching in small groups is preferable to lecturing?
[Verma and Beard, 1981, p. 113]

12a At a specific time of sustained loading, each of these lines represents the equilibrium void ratio for different values of effective overburden pressure.
[Eng2]

12b Each of these lines represents the equilibrium void ratio for different values of effective overburden pressure at a specific time of sustained loading.
[Bjerrum, 1967, p. 92]

It is important not only that language was repeated from sources without attribution, but also to understand how prevalent it was. Three measures can help put repeated language in perspective. The first is the proportion of unattributed repetition in each writing sample, arrived at by dividing the number of words which appear in the source by the number of words in each sample (excluding signalled quotation). The passage in (13) consists of 62 words, 58 of which appear in the corresponding passage in the source, so the proportion of repeated language is 58/62 = 94 per cent. (The Appendix has full details of the conventions used for this part of the analysis.)

13a Mannan which is a major constituent of the cell wall in C. albicans, inhibits a Candida antigen-induced in vitro proliferation of normal lymphocytes and also blocks the antigen-presenting ability of macrophages (Fischer et al., 1982). In addition, the polysaccharide fractions from C. albicans stimulate T-cells to produce a suppressor factor, which inhibits interleukin 1 and interleukin 2 production (Lombardi et al., 1985).

[Sci2]

13b Manna, a major constituent of the cell wall in C. albicans, was detected in the serum of some patients with mucocutaneous candidiasis (Fischer et al., 1978). Mannan inhibited a Candida antigen-induced in vitro proliferation of normal lymphocytes and also blocked the antigen-presenting ability of macrophages (Fischer et al., 1982).// In another study, polysaccharide fractions (containing mostly mannose and glucose residues) from C. albicans stimulated the T-cells to produce a suppressor factor, which in turn inhibited interleukin 1 and interleukin 2 production (Lombardi et al., 1985).

[Datta et al. 1989, p. 70]

Across the entire corpus, 23 per cent of the language of the student texts (excluding explicit quotation) can be found in the sources. This figure, however, includes some parts of the writing samples which could not be compared to a source. In some cases no comparison was possible because no source was cited, and the passage was presumably original to the student. However, in other cases a cited source was not adequately identified, or could not be obtained. The 23 per cent figure, therefore, almost certainly understates the degree of similarity between the student writing and its sources. That can be adjusted for by making the same calculation only for the portions of the student texts which were compared (and, again, not signalled as a quotation). The proportion of repeated language then rises to 41 per cent. That is, 41 per cent of the language in the compared passages of the writing samples came without attribution from the students' sources.

Because of the uncertain status of the uncompared passages, the real figure is likely to lie somewhere between these two but it is impossible to determine where. It is, however, fair to say that a significant proportion of the student texts consisted of language repeated from sources, but not indicated as quotation. When acknowledged quotation is included in the calculation, the similarity between the student texts and their sources rises even further, to 48 per cent. Although the acknowledged quotations did not constitute plagiarism, they do contribute to the emerging picture of a group of writers who were highly reliant on the language of their sources.

This picture is confirmed by Table 4.2, which shows the proportion of repeated language in each writing sample (including only the parts of the writing sample that were compared, and excluding quotation). In three texts more than two-thirds of the language compared came

TABLE 4.2 Unattributed repetition as a proportion of compared text, by writer.

Writer	Percentage in common with source	Writer	Percentage in common with source
Ingrid	95%	SS1	35%
Erden	73%	Kwan	32%
Roula	65%	Pierre	26%
Sci2	61%	SS2	26%
Eng1	49%	Graciela	23%
Eng2	48%	Sci1	19%
H1	43%	H2	16%
Yves	38%	Maria	7%
Helen	39%		
ALL (average)			41%

from sources, while in ten texts the figure was more than a third. However, Table 4.2 also illustrates that the writers varied a great deal in their dependence on their sources, with the proportion of repeated language ranging from Ingrid's 95 per cent to Maria's 7 per cent. Further, the writers varied in the extent to which they introduced changes to their sources. Some repeated extended chunks with few alterations if any, while others stitched together shorter extracts and made more changes to them. Table 4.3 shows for each text the longest string repeated exactly from a source.

Ingrid again figures as the most source-dependent of the writers, with a verbatim string of 102 words as the longest in her writing sample, and Maria is once again at the other end of the continuum, with a six-word string. The five writers with the highest proportion of language repeated from sources—Ingrid, Erden, Roula, Sci2 and Eng1—also have the five longest verbatim strings of text. Graciela's longest string was closest to the mean of 27:

14a This view is not shared by those who distinguish <u>that the practices appropriate in the pastoral sphere may not always be appropriate in the academic sphere (and vice versa), and even that separate organisational arrangements may be necessary</u>. (Best et al, 1983, p. 276)

[Graciela]

TABLE 4.3 Longest repeated string per writing sample.

Writer		Writer	
Ingrid	102	H1	17
Erden	70	Helen	17
Sci2	53	Yves	15
Roula	33	Pierre	9
Graciela	29	H2	8
Eng1	29	SS1	7
Eng2	21	Sci1	7
Kwan	19	Maria	6
SS2	17	Mean	27

14b For if there are academic activities and pastoral activities which derive their justification from their commitment to different aspects of 'the good', there are grounds for arguing <u>that the practices appropriate in the pastoral sphere may not always be appropriate in the academic sphere (and vice versa), and even that separate organizational arrangements may be necessary</u>.
[Best et al., 1983, p. 276]

The median was 17 words, the length of this from H1:

15a <u>Dell (1986) presents statistical evidence that the null-element is not always involved in onset or coda omissions</u>.
[H1]

15b <u>Dell (1986) has presented statistical evidence that the null-element is not always involved in onset or coda omissions</u> . . .
[Levelt, 1989, p. 224]

In Maria's text there was no instance of more than six words in a row identical to the source (16).

16a Stoll and Fink suggest that <u>a blend of pressure and support</u> is the key ingredient for effective change.
[Maria]

16b Successful implementation is influenced by many similar factors . . . Miles (1986) highlights the importance of:

- clear responsibility for orchestration
- shared control over implementation
- <u>a blend of pressure and support</u>
- sustained staff development
- early rewards for teachers.
[Stoll and Fink, 1996, p. 44]

Before turning to a third measure of repeated language, it is worth considering what can—and cannot—be concluded from these first two. Thus far it has been seen that there are similarities between the student texts and their sources. All other things being equal, it is reasonable to conclude that the greater the similarity, the greater the likelihood that the similarities are the result of copying, and not chance. Both the strength of that conclusion and the limitations on it can be demonstrated with that most democratic of linguistic corpora, Google[3].

The longest string in Pierre's text, *effect of time to failure on undrained shear strength,* was only nine words long, three times lower than the median. The expression *time to failure* produces 443,000 hits on Google, and the phrase *undrained shear strength* another 62,000 but the entire nine-word string generates no hits at all. Similarly, the longest string from SS1 was *be balanced by the strength of another.* The first phrase *the strength of another* generates 11,600 Google hits and 794,000 are found for *be balanced by* but there is not a single occurrence of all seven words together. This sheds some interesting light on the idea, often put forward by students, that there are only so many ways to say the same thing. It is true that phrases like 'time to failure' and 'be balanced by' are very common (in engineering and in everyday language, respectively), but they are quite unlikely to be combined in precisely the same way.

However, it cannot be concluded from this that the threshold for plagiarism lies somewhere below seven words; the likelihood of a short string recurring coincidentally depends not only on its length but also on its nature. This is illustrated by the longest string in the H2 sample, which was eight words long: *in the second half of the eighth century.*

17a Besides these two important invasions, there followed a third wave of invading populations from the East, the Illyrians, who arrived in northern Italy in the second half of the eighth century, causing the Proto-Latins to move to their historical homeland of Latium. . . . (cf. Buck (1904:2), Palmer (1954:39)).

[H2]

17b Besides what we may describe as the proto-Latin invasion of cremators by the northern land route and the slightly later 'Osco-Umbrian' invasion of 'inhumers' across the Adriatic, archaeologists list a third influx of people who show distinct eastern influences and whose arrival brought a knowledge of horse-riding as distinct from horse-driving and the intensification of horse-breeding[1]. The climax of this 'easternizing' influx came <u>in the second half of the eighth century</u> B.C.

[Palmer, 1954, p. 39]

Intuitively this sounds like the sort of phrase that could be expected to recur, and the Google experiment confirms this: it generates 7,740 hits. Predicting the likelihood that the same phrase will occur in two texts is not a simple matter, therefore. All kinds of discourse include formulaic language, phrases which function as units in much the same way as words do (e.g. Wray, 2002). Shorter, repeated chunks are more common than longer ones (e.g. Biber et al., 1999). However, length is not the only consideration.

A third source of evidence for repeated language can come, perhaps paradoxically, from differences in language which, coupled with similarities of content and structure, can be seen to be *changes* to the original. An example of this comes from Kwan's work. In both Kwan's text and her source, the passages below follow the same definition. Kwan attributes the definition to Popham (but not the discussion of it which follows).

18a A careful look <u>at</u> the above <u>definition</u> will enable one to find three words/<u>phrases</u> central to <u>the definition</u>, i.e., <u>'formal'</u>, which help* differentiate <u>educational evaluation from</u> day-to-day <u>informal</u> evaluation; <u>'appraisal of</u> the <u>quality'</u>, which defines the purpose of the evaluation, i.e. <u>a determination of</u> value and <u>'educational phenomena'</u>, which provides the target area for evaluation covering <u>many things, such as the goals</u> that an education programme <u>is</u> aimed at, the implementation of a design for an educational <u>programme</u> and the <u>outcomes of an</u> educational programme etc. Note that this definition will underlie the following discussion.

[Kwan] *sic*

18b Let's look more carefully <u>at</u> this <u>definition</u>. By using the <u>phrase</u> *systematic <u>educational evaluation</u>*, we are clearly trying to divorce our focus <u>from</u> the <u>informal</u>, everyday evaluative acts referred to previously. For that reason, <u>the definition</u> asserts that systematic educational evaluation is <u>formal</u>. The heart of the definition involves an *appraisal of quality* or, in other words, a determination of worth. The educational phenomena that are to be appraised/apprise can include many things, such as the outcomes of an instructional endeavor, the instructional programs that produced those outcomes, educational products used in educational efforts, or the goals to which educational efforts are addressed.

[Popham, 1988, p. 7]

At first glance the two passages are not overwhelmingly similar. However, the very differences between the two are suggestive of a close relationship, in two ways. The first is the language used. Although the language of Kwan's passage is more different from Popham's than similar to it, a relationship between the two can still be traced. So, for example, where Popham begins 'Let's look more carefully at this definition', Kwan proposes 'A careful look', and calls it 'the above definition' instead of 'this definition'. Figure 4.1 matches words and phrases from Popham's original with Kwan's rewording.

Not only is there a correspondence between different but similar phrases, the progression of ideas is essentially the same in the two passages. Both begin by saying that the previous definition of evaluation will be examined in more detail; they name three components of the definition (its emphasis on formality, the element of 'appraisal' and the object of the appraisal) and list some objects of evaluation. At this point Kwan departs somewhat from Popham's text: she identifies one target of evaluation not present in Popham's list, omits two targets from his list and moves the first on his list to the end of hers. Figure 4.2 shows the moves the two passages make and the language the writers use to make them.

Thus even in the absence of long chunks of identical language, it is possible to see relatively low levels of similar language as the result of a writing process which began with the source text and made changes to it. Each of the writing samples has at least one passage which is suggestive of this repeat-and-change process.

Despite the difficulties noted above in deducing the writing process from the finished product, two conclusions can be drawn about the language of the student texts: first, the writers were, to

Kwan	→	Popham
careful	→	carefully
look (noun)	→	look (verb)
the above definition	→	this definition
words/phrases	→	phrases
central to the definition	→	the heart of the definition
differentiate	→	divorce
day-to-day	→	everyday
i.e.	→	in other words
evaluation	→	evaluative acts
value	→	worth
covering	→	can include
which provides the target area for evaluation	→	that are to be appraised
education programme	→	instructional program
goals that an education programme is aimed at	→	goals to which educational efforts are addressed

FIGURE 4.1 *Tracing Kwan's changes.*

varying extents, dependent on the language of their sources, and secondly, most of the writers were not entirely transparent about the ways they had used the language of their sources.

Source Identity

Another element of transparent source use is that the source which was used should be identified. Readers make several assumptions related to the identity of sources:

- that if no citation appears for a given proposition, both the content and the form are original to the writer, and
- that if a source *is* cited, it is the source named that the writer actually consulted.

Move	Kwan	Popham
announce that the definition just given will be analyzed	A careful look at the above definition will enable one to find three words/phrases	Let's look more carefully at this definition.
identify formality as an element of the definition	i.e., 'formal', which help differentiate educational evaluation from day-to-day informal evaluation	By using the phrase systematic educational evaluation, we are clearly trying to divorce our focus from the informal, everyday evaluative acts referred to previously. For that reason, the definition asserts that systematic educational evaluation is formal.
identify judging quality as an element of the definition	'appraisal of the quality', which defines the purpose of the evaluation, i.e. a determination of value	The heart of the definition involves an appraisal of quality or, in other words, a determination of worth.
identify the things that can be evaluated as an element of the definition	and 'educational phenomena', which provides the target area for evaluation covering many things,	The educational phenomena that are to be appraised can include many things,
specify a possible target of evaluation	the implementation of a design for an educational programme	
specify a possible target of evaluation		the instructional programs that produced those outcomes,
specify a possible target of evaluation		educational products used in educational efforts,
specify a possible target of evaluation	such as the goals that an education programme is aimed at,	or the goals to which educational efforts are addressed.
specify a possible target of evaluation	and the outcomes of an educational programme etc.	such as the outcomes of an instructional endeavor,

FIGURE 4.2 *Parallel moves in two texts.*

A specific aspect of the second assumption relates to secondary citation, that is, a reference to a proposition from a work by Smith which the writer encountered not in Smith's work directly, but through a report of it in that of Jones. The reader assumes:

- that secondary citations are indicated ('Smith, as quoted in Jones'); if no such acknowledgement is made, the source which is named is assumed to be the one that the writer actually used.

However, unacknowledged secondary citation was common in the student corpus. This form of opaque source use is generally discouraged, since it obscures the responsibility for reported propositions, but it is not routinely categorized as plagiarism (although at least one university plagiarism policy has suggested precisely the opposite; see Pecorari, 2001). In some cases, though, when several sources are cited at second hand, the impression can indeed be given that the writer is taking credit for an act of synthesis that actually belonged to the source author. In such cases, unacknowledged secondary citation might more easily be interpreted as plagiarism. An extended example of this appears in (19) below. This passage contains five separate comments on culture from, apparently, five different sources. Each comment appears in quotation marks with a source named, and the impression is given that Maria has read the five sources (and possibly others), identified and written about the respects in which they are similar and different, and thus has produced an original synthesis of existing ideas.

> **19a** The anthropologist E. B. Tylor gives a fairly concise definition, looking at culture as "that complex whole which includes knowledge, belief, art, morals, law, custom and any other capabilities and habits acquired by man as a member of society" (Tylor, 1871); while the sociologist Matthew Arnold describes it as the "pursuit of our total perfection, by means of getting to know, on all matters which concern us, the best which has been thought and said" (Arnold, 1869). Bullivant on the other hand, discusses the notion of culture on the basis of its being "a patterned system of knowledge and conception, embodied

in symbolic and non-symbolic communication modes, which a society has evolved from the past, and progressively modifies and augments to give meaning to and cope with the present and anticipated future problems of its existence" (Bullivant, 1981). Malinowski takes this argument furthe*, attributing to culture the characteristic of constituting "a vast apparatus by which man is put in a position the better to cope with the concrete, specific problems which face him in his adaptation to his environment in the course of the satisfaction of his needs" (Malinowski, 1945). And Burtonwood will later comment that "this has been the predominant view of English anthropology and it has regularly found its way into introductory texts in the sociology of education" (Burtonwood, p. 3)

[Maria 1:5b]* sic

19b The first and perhaps still the best-known, and certainly the most often quoted social scientific definition of culture in English, is that of the anthropologist E. B. Tylor, who referred to 'that complex whole which includes knowledge, belief, art, morals, law, custom and any other capabilities and habits acquired by man as a member of society' (Tylor, 1871, p. 1). Two years earlier in Culture and Anarchy Matthew Arnold (1869, p. viii) had said of culture that it was 'a pursuit of our total perfection by means of getting to know, on all matters which concern us, the best which has been thought and said'. . . . The following quotation from Bullivant's discussion of educational responses to the plurality of cultures within societies indicates how the notion of culture now taken on board by educationists is emphatically that of the anthropologist:

Culture is a patterned system of knowledge and conception, embodied in symbolic and non-symbolic communication modes, which a society has evolved from the past, and progressively modifies and augments to give meaning to and cope with the present and anticipated future problems of its existence. (Bullivant, 1981, p. 3). . . . Malinowski (1945, p. 42), for instance saw culture as 'the whole body of implements, the charters of its social groups, human ideas, beliefs and customs' and it 'constitutes a vast apparatus by which man is put in a position the better to cope with the concrete,

> specific problems which face him in his adaptation to his environment in the course of the satisfaction of his needs'. This has been the predominant view of English anthropology and it has regularly found its way into introductory texts in the sociology of education.
>
> [Burtonwood, 1986, pp. 2–3]

In fact, however, the final source Maria names, Burtonwood, cites the other four writers, for precisely the same definitions of culture, in the same order as Maria. It is difficult to dispute the conclusion that Maria has based her passage on Burtonwood. Even if Maria actually consulted each of the other four sources, the original idea of bringing them together was not hers. It is apparent that in spite of her care to observe quotation marks (extending even to language which seems to be Burtonwood's paraphrase of Bullivant, rather than a quotation from Bullivant as Maria makes it appear) Maria has obscured the identity of her source.

This passage from Maria's writing sample is not typical; it is the longest example of unattributed secondary citation in the corpus. However, wherever it occurs, the effect of unattributed secondary citation is to make the actual relationship between the report of a source and the way the writer used the source opaque, and it was found in all of the writing samples except H2[4].

Apart from unacknowledged secondary citation, other inaccuracies in identifying sources arose. An important source in Maria's writing sample was an edited volume, and Maria consistently cited the editors, rather than the authors of the individual papers. When this was combined with unacknowledged secondary citation, the actual source was two removes away from the one cited, as in (20a), where the words in quotation marks are credited to Fullan and Hargreaves, but came in fact from van Mannen, who was quoted in a chapter by Grimmet and Crehan, which appeared in a volume edited by Fullan and Hargreaves.

20a An interesting characteristic of culture as Fullan and Hargreaves put it, questions the concretness* of the above definition, as they both claim that <u>culture is</u> invisible. However, they do take the argument even further to explain that <u>culture is</u> indeed invisible "but it is made visible only through its representation" (Fullan and Hargreaves, pp. 58–60).

[Maria]* sic

20b 'Culture is not itself visible, but is made visible only through its representation' (Van Mannen, 1988:3). Culture is constructed reality. It is known by its representation.
[Grimmett and Crehan, 1992, pp. 58–59, in Fullan and Hargreaves]

In some cases there simply was no reference clearly intended to apply to a proposition which from one of the sources. Sometimes this was due to the awkward placement of a reference giving a misleading impression about what it was intended to cover. In (21a) the source for the entire excerpt is Lakoff and Johnson, but it is not clear that the first sentence of the passage is included in the citation's coverage.

21a Metaphor is for most people a feature of extraordinary rather than ordinary language. According to Lakoff and Johnson (1980: 3) metaphor is typically viewed as a characteristic of language alone, a matter of words rather than thought or action. For this reason, most people think they can get along perfectly well without metaphor.
[Roula]

21b Metaphor is for most people a device of the poetic imagination and the rhetorical flourish—a matter of extraordinary rather than ordinary language. Moreover, metaphor is typically viewed as characteristic of language alone, a matter of words rather than thought or action. For this reason, most people think they can get along perfectly well without metaphor.
[Lakoff and Johnson, 1980, p. 3]

In other cases there was simply no citation which could reasonably be thought to apply to material which had evidently come from a source, as in (22).

22a Sensitivity, S, is usually defined as the ratio between the undisturbed shear strength to the remoulded shear strength, as determined either from vane test or from unconfined compression test. The larger this ratio is, the more sensitive is the clay. Normally consolidated clay very often exhibits sensitivity values of 1.0 to 4.0 and in some cases up to 8.0. Heavily overconsolidated clays and most boulder clays are insensitive, S = 1.0.

[Eng2]

22b Sensitivity, St, is usually defined as the ratio of the undisturbed shear strength to the remoulded shear strength, determined either from vane tests or from unconfined compression tests.//Sensitivities of 2 to 4 are very common among normally consolidated clays, and even sensitivities of 4 to 8 are frequently encountered. Heavily overconsolidated clays and most boulder clays are insensitive (St ≈ 1.0) (Skempton and Northey, 1952).

[Brenner et al., 1981, pp. 214–215]

In still other cases, inaccuracies appeared in the reference list. These ranged from sources which were not included in the reference list, to entries which contained more or less serious inaccuracies, or which omitted important details. For example, Yves' thesis reported tests on two products which could be used to improve unpaved roads, and he referred frequently to information provided by the manufacturers of those products. One of his reference list entries (in his completed thesis) reads 'Roadtech 2000—Manufacturer information'. Without his help and that of his supervisor it would have been impossible to obtain his sources, a fact which highlights why wrong or incomplete source identification is a problem. There is no reason to believe that these writers wanted to conceal information about their sources; the problems are much more likely to be due to factors such as oversight (e.g. in the case of missing reference list entries) or unfamiliarity with conventions (in the case, for example, of unattributed secondary citation).

Nonetheless, the writers' responsibility was to identify all of their sources transparently, and many did not do so. The individual texts varied greatly in the extent of opaque source use and in the types of problems that were found. For example, Ingrid's writing sample consisted of 19 passages, 8 of which did not cite any source at all, although they were nearly identical to passages from her sources.

By comparison, there were no parts of Maria's texts which lacked a citation where one could be shown to be needed, but in six passages she gave the wrong source. Roula cited the wrong source twice and omitted a citation where one was needed three times, but in six places had a reference to the correct source placed so that it was not at all clear that she intended the reference to cover all of the material from that source, as in (21a), above. The writers varied, therefore, in the types of problems they had in identifying their sources. However, among all the writing samples, only H2 can be said to have declared its sources unambiguously throughout.

Transparent Report of Content

The third area in which transparency must be achieved is the content of the reported proposition. The writer's responsibility here is to report material from sources accurately. Readers assume, quite simply, that the content attributed to a source is accurate and undistorted. In this area as well, the writers were not always transparent. One circumstance in which this happened was when the writers attempted to paraphrase or reword a source. In (23a) Graciela quotes from Watkins about the contribution that pastoral care (PC) makes to education. In introducing her quotation she moves away from Watkins' language, and in doing so changed Watkins' claim: what he had identified as a *specific* contribution becomes the *main* contribution.

23a Watkins (1985) <u>says that the</u> main <u>contribution of PC</u> may <u>be</u> that it <u>brings 'attention to the personal and interpersonal dimensions and to give a pupil-centred focus'</u> (p. 179).

[Graciela]

23b The broad ambition of pastoral care is to help pupils benefit more extensively from their school experience. But this is surely the broad aim of any school, so is it worth saying? Yes, if we go on to <u>say that the</u> more specific <u>contribution of pastoral care is</u> to <u>bring attention to the personal and interpersonal dimensions, and to give a pupil-centred focus</u>.

[Watkins, 1985, p. 179]

It is interesting to note that the concern voiced by students in some studies of writing (e.g. Angélil-Carter, 2000; see Chapter 2) is a real one: the effort to paraphrase carries with it a risk of distorting the source. Roula also changed the meaning of one of her sources along with some changes to the language (24). Stern (cited in Black, a secondary citation that Roula did not acknowledge) compares figures of speech to non-figurative language. Roula, however, says that he compares metaphor to other figures of speech. Here it is difficult not to wonder whether the distortion actually sprang from Roula misunderstanding her source. If so, this underscores the fundamental relationship between good reading skills and good writing from sources (Howard, 2001).

24a Stern says that metaphor succeeds better than all the other figures of speech to serve the expressive and purposive functions of speech better than the plain statement (Black, 1992*).

[Roula] *sic

24b [12] Thus Stern (*op. cit.*) says of all figures of speech that "they are intended to serve the expressive and purposive functions of speech better than the 'plain statement'" (p. 296).

[Black, 1962, p. 34]

In some cases the shift of focus resulted in apparent additional support for the writer's argument. In (25b) Stoll and Fink discuss change in schools in very specific terms, arriving at a conclusion about 'what *the* change should be' (italics added). Maria makes a point about change more generally (later arguing that what Stoll and Fink said about change could be applied to another context), but to do so finds it necessary to remove Stoll and Fink's definite article (carefully inserting an ellipsis).

25a As Stoll and Fink suggest 'There is not only one version of what . . . change should be' while 'a main purpose of the process is for all involved to exchange realities and continue to develop ideas' (Stoll and Fink, p. 45)

[Maria]

25b There is not only one version of what the change should be. A main purpose of the process is for all involved to exchange realities and continue to develop ideas.

[Stoll and Fink, 1996, p. 45]

The SS2 writing sample featured some especially clear-cut misrepresentation of the sources. In the section from which the excerpt in (26) was taken, SS2 weighs the pros and cons of various social science research methods and criticizes interviews for their potential for the interviewer to influence findings. This is supported by references to several sources, including a paper by Ann Oakley, advocate of the feminist research paradigm. In the paper Oakley argues persuasively that better and richer interview data can be obtained if the researcher interacts with interview participants rather than treating them as objects of the research process, giving examples of how that has happened in her own research. While it is true, strictly speaking, that 'the interviewer may also influence the responses' as SS2 says, to call this 'bias' or imply that it is a 'limitation of the interview technique' is to misrepresent Oakley's position.

26 In relation to this, Parry (1982) noted that the interaction between respondents and the interviewer is subject to bias from many sources. For instance, the personal experience, sex, age, social status, race and ethnicity of the interviewer may also influence the responses (Oakley, 1981). . . . A further limitation of the interview technique concerns cost. Interviews are expensive (Verma & Beard, 1981; Slavin, 1974).

[SS2]

Thus in terms of the content of their sources, as well as their identity and the origins of the language used, these writers did not always present the nature of their source use transparently to their readers. Did that lack of transparency constitute plagiarism? Three criteria for deciding that question were set out at the beginning of this chapter:

1 whether there were similarities of language and/or ideas between two texts;
2 whether the similarities came about because one text drew upon another and
3 whether the intertextual relationship (if any) was signalled appropriately.

It has been seen that there were indeed similarities of language between all of the student texts and their sources, but the other two criteria are less straightforward. Whether similarities are causal requires a judgement call. Many readers will find that decision easy to make when it comes to Ingrid's 102-word-long passage repeated verbatim from her source, but other cases are less clear, and many may find—as I do—that the language that H2 shared with her source (of which 'in the second half of the eighth century' is the most substantial example) is not a clear indication of copying. With regard to the third criterion—whether the relationship was signalled appropriately—the situation is even less clear-cut. It has been shown that all of the writers failed to identify their sources unambiguously, but in that zone of ambiguity reactions are likely to be widespread. How should Roula's text be considered? It featured references placed so that much of the material that patently came from the sources was not clearly attributed to them, yet, the references were largely present. Moreover, some academic writers would argue that repeating language from a source without attribution is appropriate, in some circumstances (Flowerdew and Li, 2007), so the absence of any citation at all may not necessarily be inappropriate. What is clear, though, is that all of these writers used sources in such a way that *could* lay them open to an accusation of plagiarism. Chapter 2 illustrated the damage that even an accusation of plagiarism can do, and none of these writers was entirely safe from that risk.

The other perspective that must be considered is whether the opacity surrounding much of the source use in these texts occurred as a result of intentional deception. This point will be considered in Chapter 5. First, though, the next section will move beyond the question of whether the source use was appropriate, and consider whether it was effective.

Were Sources Used to Good Effect?

In Chapter 1 it was seen that one explanation that has been offered for (some) textual plagiarism is the writer's experience or skill level. The lack of experience and skills is likely to be seen in other aspects of source use than textual plagiarism, or in other features of the text generally. This section presents a detailed examination of the source use, and of the other textual skills, of two writers, H2 and SS2. As was seen in the previous section, H2 was quite transparent about her source use[5]. Her text contained the second-lowest proportion of language from sources, and only short strings of verbatim text. She was also more consistent than the other writers about identifying her sources and reporting their content faithfully. SS2, on the other hand, failed to achieve transparency in all three areas (although he was not at the extreme opposite end of the continuum). Does their respective success or lack thereof in transparent source use mirror their skills in writing from sources more generally? To answer that question, this section will consider (1) the purpose of their texts, and how effectively it was put forward; (2) the purpose for which individual citations were used; (3) their success in matching the formal aspects of citations with their purposes and (4) the interaction between the purpose of citation and the repetition of language from sources.

Sense of Overall Purpose

One of the most striking differences between the two texts is the sense in H2 that the writing sample has a role to fill in the larger text, and that each move advances that purpose. This sense of connection and relevance is largely missing from the SS2 sample. The difference is evident from as early as the first paragraphs. The H2 thesis describes the language variety spoken in the Italian region of Calabria. The chapter from which the writing sample comes is entitled 'Calabria: the historical background', and in the first paragraph the writer states that to understand 'the present-day linguistic situation in Calabria' it is also necessary to understand the history of the region, and in particular the movement of people and languages in and out of the area. Little argument is needed for the idea that the way people speak today has historical roots, so it is easy to accept the writer's assertion that the review will be useful.

> **27** The present-day region of Calabria is characterized by a notable degree of linguistic fragmentation, a situation which has come about as a result of the various movements of a number of diverse ethnic groups and populations which, at various times, have settled alongside each other within the region. Consequently, in order to gain a better understanding of the present-day linguistic situation in Calabria, it is necessary to chart the historical episodes which characterized this region, establishing, in particular, the ancient populations and languages which preceded the eventual widespread expansion of a number of Romance dialects. It is to this question that we now turn.
>
> [H2]

In the pages that follow, it is clear how the material presented advances the writer's purpose. In part this is achieved through the same means as in (27): the discussion is manifestly relevant to the purpose of the chapter and its role in advancing the argument of the thesis, so little explanation is needed. But H2 diligently connects this section with the larger text, reminding the reader of the direction being taken. One strategy is making direct reference to the topic of the thesis. Given the focus of the chapter and the topic of the thesis as a whole, to establish relevance the writer must establish two sets of connections: between events in the region and the language spoken there, which was done explicitly in (27), and between Calabria's past and its present. To accomplish the latter, H2 frequently concludes paragraphs of historical description with a reminder that the present is her focus.

> **28 In present-day Italy,** the wide-spread diffusion of Italian has been such that the use of Greek is **now** restricted to a number of villages . . .
>
> [H2] (emphasis added)

29 One final point of note concerns the fact that, although the former predominance of Greek is now seriously diminished within **present-day Calabria** . . .

[H2] (emphasis added)

30 Although the fate of the Greek dialects spoken in **present-day Calabria** appears to be somewhat bleak . . .

[H2] (emphasis added)

On a larger scale, the historical data are connected to the current situation by means of a section over three pages long describing 'some of the morphosyntactic features of the Romance dialects of southern Calabria which can be presumably attributed to Greek intermediacy, inasmuch as these same features surface in the modern *Grìco* dialects' (i.e. features of modern dialects which are the result of historical Greek influences).

In addition, metatextual references serve to remind the reader of the larger context:

31 As will be discussed **in chapter 3** in greater detail . . . .

[H2] (emphasis added)

32 In order to aid the general understanding of examples discussed **in the main body of the present thesis** . . .

[H2] (emphasis added)

33 Finally, limits of space are such that inclusion of area 1 **in the present thesis** . . .

[H2] (emphasis added)

The reader is, therefore, constantly reminded that the information reviewed in this chapter is provided for a purpose, painting a backdrop which will allow the research data presented in later chapters to be understood.

SS2 also asserts a connection between the chapter and the thesis: by explaining the research methods and the reasons for choosing them, the way is prepared for the reader to understand the findings presented later in the thesis.

34 The present chapter sets out and seeks to justify the research design employed to examine the current state of teaching [*specific topic and context omitted*]. It also considers the factors implicated in that design and the circumstances under which the fieldwork was conducted. Thus, it prepares the ground for the following two chapters in which the data generated from it are presented. However, the purpose of the present chapter is to provide the reader with an insight into the research techniques adopted in the collection of data for the fieldwork element of the study.

Both writers have used in their first paragraphs (27 and 34) what has been termed 'advanced labelling', with which 'the writer both labels and commits him/herself to perform a discourse act' (Tadros, 1994, p. 73). Unfortunately, with the next paragraph, SS2 takes a step away from honouring that commitment by announcing a broad review of research methods in the field:

35 It was decided to give a brief description of the different types of educational research with a view to justifying the techniques adopted in the present study. The previous literature helped the researcher to gain an insight into the strategies adopted by other researchers seeking to obtain similar educational data. This made a significant contribution to the design of the study. Thus, before discussing the research design, it is necessary to outline the literature concerning research and research methods widely used in education. This may also help to justify the suitability of the methods adopted for the present research.

The need for this approach is described in terms of the writer's processes; his reading about educational research methods gave him an understanding from which he could develop his own methods. His assertion that he must explain his progress to be able to report his conclusions is an example of writer-based prose (Flower, 1979).

Thus, in the first paragraph the H2 sample has promised a historical review and shown the purpose it will serve in the larger text. The SS2 text, on the other hand, has promised a literature review but has merely asserted, not demonstrated, the need for it. The literature review is delivered, covering three areas: definitions of the term 'research'; general approaches to research in the social sciences and specific research methods. The discussion is carried out at a general level, with few direct links to the thesis topic. Indeed, in places the text positively invites a connection to the research reported in the field, but the writer sidesteps it. For example, in several places the idea is asserted that no research method is intrinsically better than another. Since 'all methods of research have their own strengths and weaknesses', the choice of a research method should be decided by 'the ultimate aim of a study'. Here the writer reaches for an example, and it seems only natural to expect that the aims of *his* study will be introduced. Instead, the example chosen is abstract and unrelated to the thesis:

36 As an example, if the problem of a study is related to medicine, an experimental approach would probably be suitable. If, on the other hand, the problem of a study is historical in its nature, then the most appropriate method of enquiry could be historical.

This strategy of keeping the chapter's topic and that of the thesis at arm's length continues until, seven pages into the chapter, the writer states 'because of the nature of the present research, the researcher elected to use descriptive and survey methods'. There is no explanation of which aspects of the research dictated those methods. The previous pages, which discussed the pros and cons of various methods and repeated that none is good or bad in itself but must be chosen in relation to the topic, suddenly appear irrelevant. Throughout the rest of the text, methodological choices are announced as something that 'was decided' without justifying them by connecting them to what came before, or to the wider topic.

In summary, H2 succeeded in connecting her writing sample to the thesis as a whole in part by reporting content which was clearly relevant to her topic, but also did not neglect the rhetorical task of pointing up the relevance to the reader. SS2 not only chose to devote space to matters of questionable relevance, but also was not an effective advocate for his own work. SS2, it appears, does not have clear reasons for a lengthy description of research methods: they were reviewed because, like the famous mountain, they were there. He made promises about his intentions which were ultimately not kept, thus undermining his authority. In this respect, H2 has shown herself to be a more skilful writer than SS2.

Citation Purpose

Citations can serve many purposes, some of which were outlined in Chapter 3. An important overarching principle, though, is that they should serve *some* purpose. In one of his language commentaries on National Public Radio's programme *Fresh Air*, the linguist Geoff Nunberg had this to say about Lynn Truss' book on punctuation: 'she tosses semi-colons into her sentences in something like the way I scatter fennel seed when I'm cooking: in the vague hope it'll somehow pull the other ingredients together' (2005). This is one of the key differences between the two writing samples: while H2 cited sources selectively to advance her purposes, the SS2 text scattered references as if they were fennel seed.

This does not make SS2 an unusual academic writer. Integrating sources with each other and with the larger argument is an essential task in constructing an academic text, but the skills required to do so, synthesizing items from the literature critically and reporting them in relationship to each other, are challenging for many inexperienced writers (Richards, 1988, p. 197). In a study of novice and expert writers, Geisler concluded of one of the novices that

> . . . her claims stand in ambiguous relationships to the claims of the authors she is opposing. She does not, for example, make clear how her own definition of paternalism relates to her definitions she reviews earlier. Is it in agreement? Is it in disagreement? Is it a qualified agreement? She is not clear. . . . Structurally, what is lacking here is the critique used so extensively by both experts. Instead of an argument structure that eliminates other authors' approaches on the way to validating her own, Novice 2 simply presents the two approaches side by side. . . .
>
> (1991, pp. 180–181)

Such writing emerges with 'no coherent argument at all, but a mere arrangement of summaries of antecedent texts, stitched together without any discernible overarching writerly purpose' (Groom, 2000, p. 17).

This was the sort of source reporting found in the SS2 sample. Nineteen of the thirty-seven sources cited there were books about research in education or the social sciences. Not surprisingly, there was considerable overlap in the content dealt with in these volumes, and it was not unusual for SS2 to refer to two or more in the same citation, or in neighbouring citations. This was ordinarily done, though, with no comment on the relationship among them, or between them and his argument. Indeed, such clues as are provided by linking words and expressions, etc., are often more confusing than enlightening. The passage in (37) refers to two sources and reports ideas which partly overlap and are partly different, as shown in Figure 4.3.

37 However, Mason and Bramble (1978) argued that "historical research can offer a clearer perspective on the present, and that it can also be useful for future predictions". In addition to this, some writers such as Fox and Tobias (1969) noted that historical research is a past oriented research which seeks to throw light on current conditions and problems through an intensive study of materials and information which already exist.

[SS2]

Both sources identify historical research as informing about the present. In addition, Fox (the student's reference to Fox and Tobias is an error) highlights the fact that historical research has its roots in the past, while Mason and Bramble say that it can also inform about the future. These two sources are linked by 'in addition', which tends to highlight the proposition from Fox that is different (what Fox says that is additional to what Mason and Bramble said), consequently bringing the idea raised by both sources out of focus. Yet if that idea is not of

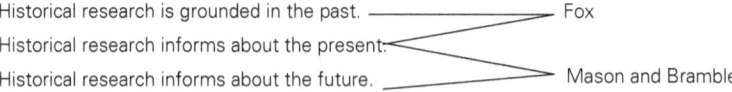

FIGURE 4.3 *Propositional content in two source reports.*

central interest, why repeat it, when that ground has already been covered by Mason and Bramble? As a result it is unclear how the two source reports are meant to work jointly to achieve the writer's purposes.

How could the writer have presented the propositions from the two sources more effectively? To answer that would require understanding the writer's objectives, but several options were available, including highlighting similarities and differences between the sources, as in (38), or shifting the emphasis selectively, as in (39) and (40).

38 Historical research places, as Fox (1969) notes, an emphasis on the past, using existing materials to inform the present. However, historical research can go beyond illuminating the present and even help predict the future (Mason & Bramble, 1978).

39 Historical research is, as Fox (1969) notes, past-oriented, and makes use of existing documents and information; however, the results can provide information about current situations (Fox, 1969; Mason & Bramble, 1978).

40 There is wide agreement that historical research can inform present situations and problems (e.g. Fox, 1969). In addition, Mason and Bramble argue, it can help predict the future (1978).

Each of those three versions has a different focus. Possibly none of them achieves what SS2 hoped to by citing them; his objectives were not clear.

By contrast, H2 is more skilful in showing the relationship between sources.

41 First, there already exist a number of rather detailed studies of the dialects of area 1 (c.f. Rohlfs (1966, 1968, 1969), Lausberg (1939), and Trumper (1979)), whereas the dialects of areas 2, 3 and 4 have, on the whole, traditionally attracted less attention from linguists.

[H2]

The relationship between the five sources named is that all are studies of area 1; the purpose in naming them is to support the assertion that area 1 has been investigated in 'a number of . . . studies'. For the most part the H2 sample reports historical data which are presented as uncontested and straightforward, but in a few instances a scholarly disagreement is reported:

> **42** In the wake of such recent studies as Trumper, Maddalon, Chiodo (1995), Trumper & Lombardi (1996), Trumper (1997) and Trumper, Chiodo and Guerra (1995), the traditional Rohlfsian thesis which dissects Calabria into two distinct linguistic areas, namely *Calabria citra* (or Latin Calabria) to the north and *Calabria ultra* (Greek Calabria) to the south, is now generally held to be inadequate.
>
> *[H2]*

The relationship among the sources is clear: Trumper and the others cited versus Rohlfs and those unnamed others who have taken the traditional view.

In much the same way that H2 was seen to construct an argument while SS2 merely reported facts (with a connection to the thesis which was tenuous at best), H2 has deployed citations tactically to support her argument, while SS2 has simply listed them.

Formal Citation Features

H2 has been more effective in using citation to achieve her purposes. What about the formal features of citation? In Chapter 2 it was seen that a basic choice writers must make is between integral citations, in which the name of the source author appears as an element in the citing sentence, and non-integral citations, in which the source author is relegated to a parenthetical reference. The effect of integral citations is often to give the source author considerable prominence in the new text, sometimes equal to or even greater than the proposition for which the citation is given. Integral citations tend to enhance the authority of the source, often to the detriment of the writer's.

The two writers differed greatly in their preferred form of incorporation. SS2 made more frequent references to sources than H2. His text contained 71 source mentions (counting each naming of each source separately), to H2's 50, in spite of the fact that H2's text is approximately 30 per cent longer than SS2's. Of SS2's 71 source mentions, 45, or 63 per cent, are integral (43), while the majority of H2's (37, or 74 per cent) are non-integral (44).

> **43** According to Verma and Beard (1981), <u>research is an organized effort to</u> obtain <u>new information or to utilize existing information for a specific and new purpose</u>.
>
> [SS2]
>
> **44** By this time, much of Calabria had already been subject to considerable Greek <u>colonisation</u> under the Chaldicians and the Achaeans, who <u>had begun</u> to colonize <u>southern Italy and Sicily</u> during <u>the eighth century BC</u> (Palmer (1954:49ff.)).
>
> [H2]

In (44) the writer confidently asserts the proposition, with Palmer's additional support, and the effect is to position her as knowledgeable on her topic. In (43), though, responsibility for the proposition is given to the source, casting SS2 in the less authoritative role of a reporter.

The tendency of integral citations to allocate greater prominence, and thus authority, to the source than to the writer can be overridden, as in (45) where the use of 'as' signals evaluation:

> **45** As noted by Rohlfs (1969:§639), this use of the *dativo greco* is paralleled by a number of the dialects spoken in the extreme south of Calabria . . .
>
> [H2]

'As noted by Rohlfs' means, in effect, 'Rohlfs notes and is right to do so', and by evaluating Rohlfs as being correct, the writer confers on herself at least equal authority to Rohlfs. The same evaluative effect would have been created if the sentence following (43) had begun 'however', and had been followed with a criticism of the source. The authority-stripping effect of integral citations can also be neutralized when they are introduced to support an idea that has been averred by the writer, rather than attributed to another source, as in (46).

> **46** Unfortunately for the linguist, today within Calabria *Grecanico,* or *Grìco* as it is called by its speakers, presently finds itself in

an irrevocably precarious position and is almost certain to die out within the near future. For instance, Rohlfs (1977:XIX-XX) claims that in the villages of Bova, Condofuri and Roccaforte, *Grìco* continues to be spoken only by a small number of speakers . . .

[H2]

Of the 13 integral source mentions in H2's text, 4 appear in the form of 'as X notes' or 'for example, x notes', while only two of SS2's 45 integral source mentions do (one of which is shown in 47, below).

Because integral citations make the source author prominent, they are useful when the point to be made is that disagreement or consensus exists on a topic. That use also is less limiting to the writer's authority, since the writer is drawing on the sources not merely to report a proposition, but to report propositions in relation to each other, as was the case in (42). It was that sort of authority that SS2 often seemed to be aiming for with references such as the ones in (47).

47 Questionnaires can be used to obtain information about current conditions and practices and to ascertain attitudes and opinions about an issue, object or situation (Lovell and Lawson, 1970). In addition, as Ary and his associates (1979) suggested, they tend to be used to explore attitudes and opinions about certain issues, objects and situations.

[SS2]

However, in this extract and generally in SS2's text, the effect is weakened by the fact that, as in (37), the writer only *superficially* shows sources in relation to each other. Here again, two sources are referred to, the second being introduced with 'in addition'. The second citation could position the writer as sufficiently authoritative to know what 'Ary and his associates' can add to what Lovell and Lawson said. The effect is marred, though, by the fact that not a great deal is added. Lovell and Lawson say that questionnaires can provide information about:

- 'current conditions and practices'
- 'attitudes and opinions about an issue, object or situation'

Ary et al. say that questionnaires can provide information about:

- 'attitudes and opinions about certain issues, objects and situations'

This highlights the point which was made earlier but deserves repeating: manipulating formal aspects of citations is an important skill for the academic writer, but form has to follow function. The problem with SS2's text is not that the writer simply made less effective formal choices in citation, but that those choices—like 'in addition' to introduce a source which does not in fact add anything to the first—are not matched to a clear purpose for the citations.

The final formal citation feature that will be considered in this section is the choice of reporting verb. The SS2 text contained more reporting verbs than H2 (not surprisingly, given that it also contained more integral citations). However, higher frequency did not yield greater variety; SS2's sources *argue* something eight times, *note* six times, *mention* five times, *emphasize* four times and *see* and *define* twice each. In the H2 text *note, observe* and *see* appear twice each, and all other reporting verbs are used once only.

Here again, though, which reporting verbs were used is less important than how they were used in relation to the purpose of the citation. Unsurprisingly by now, H2 selects reporting verbs that advance the local or global purpose of the text. In (48) H2 reports 'a matter of controversy'. When she causes her source to *argue* for his position, the reader's awareness of the controversy makes it clear why Rohlfs has to *argue*, as opposed to (for example) *stating* or *reporting*.

> **48** What remains a matter of controversy, though, is whether . . . Rohlfs ([1972] 1997) adheres to the former of these two hypotheses, arguing that . . .
>
> [H2]

By contrast, SS2's reporting verbs appear to be less the result of active discrimination than random choice. The ideas in (49) and (50)—for example that researchers should use 'a range of methods' and that they should be 'suitable', or that personality is complex—do not appear, on the face of it, to need much argument.

49 In addition to this, Burgess (1984) argued that the researcher should follow a range of methods that are suitable to his research, needing to be flexible in his approach, and to be prepared to use a range of methods in order to deal with complex problems.

[SS2]

50 (a) Lovell and Lawson (1970) who argued that an individual's total personality is exceedingly complex and the questionnaire is impersonal.

[SS2]

Source Language and Citation Purpose

This comparison of features of the two writing samples has shown that in a number of respects H2 was the more skilful writer, and that much of her success was due to the fact that she had a sense of purpose and brought into her text only those elements which would serve it. The SS2 text, on the other hand, looks backward to the existing literature rather than forward to what can be achieved by building upon it. It reports content from sources but does not use the content as a tool for advancing a textual purpose. Importantly, the relative skill of the two writers bears a connection to their use of language from their sources.

The suggestion that dependence on source language can be a function of a writer's skill is a familiar one, and several effects of skill on source use have been explored thus far. Less skilled writers may fear that by paraphrasing they can distort the content of the source. They may have a narrower range of rhetorical devices at their disposal (it is possible that SS2's inappropriate *in additions* entered the text because he did not have other, better alternatives to hand). Novice writers may feel unable to produce smooth, academic-sounding prose on their own.

All of these are contributing factors to source-dependent language; yet another is the sense of purpose that H2 had and

SS2 apparently lacked. In the absence of a clear direction for the text, it is easier to integrate material from a source in its original form; the source author's choices will not clash with the objectives of the new text, because those do not exist or are only weakly formulated. By contrast, the more experienced writer who refers to sources selectively wants to highlight those aspects of the source which are most relevant to the argument in the citing text, and it becomes, therefore, more difficult to adopt the language of the source as well as its ideas. The extract from H2's text in (51a) illustrates this.

> **51a** As for Magna Graecia, despite the eventual political overthrow and fall of Magna Graecia to the Roman Empire, Rome displayed no intention of suppressing the long-established Hellenic linguistic tradition, as observed by Pulgram 1958: 280), who states that <u>'Rome's aims were not linguistic but military and political'</u>.
>
> *[H2]*

This extract comes from a section which documents the presence of Greek in the dialect area studied in the thesis. The relevance of the Roman empire to this discussion is that the decline of Greek influence and the rise of Roman power might well have resulted in Greek being wiped out, but did not. The quotation presents the reason why that did not happen (the Romans were not primarily interested in linguistic domination). An examination of the passage from which the quotation was drawn (51b) shows that it could not have been longer without shifting H2's focus.

> **51b** ... previous to the Social War, Roman territory did not constitute a compact block from whose confines Romanization pushed forward, eating progressively into new territory, but it is made up outside of Latium of a number of islands from which the military and civil Romanization radiates in all directions until its circles of influence meet and overlap. I should compare this type of expansion with the spreading of waves in a pool: by throwing in one rock, the waves will emanate from this center and slowly and with decreasing strength spread over the entire

surface; but by throwing in several rocks in succession at strategic spots, the movement of the waves will more quickly and efficiently cover a wider area. Since linguistic spread is often likened to such wave formations, the simile illustrates how the Latinization of Italy could be more rapid and profound by issuing from a number of foci rather than from one. Of course, <u>Rome's aims were not linguistic but military and political</u>, but there is no doubt that the strategy is eminently sound for this purpose, too. (It was, by the way, employed in the Second World War in the occupation by the United States of the immense area of the Pacific Ocean and was commonly known as 'island hopping.')

[Pulgram, 1958, p. 280]

Pulgram's point in this passage is a fundamentally different one from H2's. He is concerned with the spread of the Roman territory, and describes how an 'island hopping' approach facilitated the rapid spread of Latin. (This does not contradict H2, who did not claim that Latin did not gain influence in the area, but merely that it did not wipe out the Greek variety.) The nine-word quotation—one of the very few in the H2 sample—is equally true in both texts, but does something different for each. Were the quotation to be extended at either end, it would no longer be a good fit for the H2 passage either in form or in content. This illustrates how the language one author intended for a given purpose is likely to be an uncomfortable fit for a new purpose in a new text, possibly one reason why quotation is less often used than other forms of incorporation. By implication, texts which have a clear sense of purpose are less likely to include a large proportion of repeated language in any form, whether properly attributed quotation or textual plagiarism, because merging the author's voice with the writer's is a difficult task. By contrast, texts without a clear sense of purpose lack that natural resistance to textual plagiarism.

In a study of two writers in the process of revising texts for a new purpose, Hewings and Houghton identified two strikingly different approaches, **'rephrasing,** where the revision process is text-based, and . . . **reconceptualisation,** where the starting point is the perceived needs of the audience' (1992, p. 106; emphasis in the original). The writer who adopted a rephrasing approach moved 'almost identical sections' (1992, p. 120) from one piece of his writing to another. The writer who used reconceptualization strategies produced a text which was both less similar to the original and more successful for the new purpose. There is no implication—by Houghton and Hewings, or here—that the rephrasing process constituted textual plagiarism, but a parallel exists in the repetition of language from one text to another. A clear sense of purpose for a new text motivates fundamental textual changes. In the absence of that motivation, there is no reason why language which was good enough once should not be good enough a second time.

The absence of a purpose, a sense of direction, suggests the absence of a sense of an authorial identity. That is, a writer who does not know what direction a text should take may not perceive him- or herself as someone with sufficient authority to decide on that direction, or as having the responsibility to do so. Such a writer will, almost inevitably, perceive the authority of published sources as greater than his or her own. Abasi et al. (2006) looked at the source use of five postgraduate second-language writers and found that for two of them the lack of a sense of authority over their texts and in relation to their sources was a cause of textual plagiarism.

> Both Mina and Parvin would have been able to construct an authorial identity had they appropriated materials from sources and populated them with their own intentions, and adapted them to their own unique rhetorical purposes. Mina and Parvin's view of sources as authoritative rather than internally persuasive prevented them from entering into a dialogic interaction with source texts to generate new meanings. This ultimately undermined their author(ity) in the sense of having something to say. . . . Neither of these two student writers had [an] epistemological relation to their sources and, therefore, tended to merely retell what they were reading in their own texts. This retelling approach coupled with their erratic documentation skills ultimately constructed them as plagiarists.
>
> (p. 112)

That description of Mina and Parvin's relationship to their work offers an attractive explanation for some of the differences between the H2 and SS2 texts. H2 comes across in her thesis as confident, knowledgeable and 'having something to say', while SS2's apparent lack of authority led both to the sorts of retellings that Mina and Parvin produced, and to textual plagiarism.

This chapter has examined the source use in 17 texts produced by postgraduate writers. The writers varied greatly in their individual approaches to source use, but a clear tendency in the corpus was that source use was often not signalled transparently. It is difficult to conclude which aspects of the source use problems deserve to be called plagiarism, but any of the texts in this corpus could have attracted that label. How the writers themselves account for their source use will be the focus of the next chapter, and how their texts were received by their disciplinary communities will be addressed in Chapter 6.

Notes

1. Terms for the extended pieces of research writing done by postgraduate students vary; here *thesis* will be used for the work of both the master's and the PhD students. The terms *advisor* and *supervisor* are used interchangeably here to refer to the member of the department teaching staff with primary responsibility for directing each student's research and thesis writing.
2. Attempts at quantifying the degree of similarity that indicates plagiarism have been made. For example, Turrell (2004) makes a valuable contribution towards providing a benchmark figure in the specific context of translation. The considerations that arise in her analysis illustrate, however, the context-sensitive nature of the endeavour. Even if a robust threshold value existed for one type of academic text, it would not be safe to assume that it can be applied to other text types or within other disciplines.
3. See Coulthard (2004) for a similar application of this Googling strategy, and Nunberg (2006, pp. 215–216) for a discussion of some problems in using search engines for linguistic research. The searches mentioned in this section were carried out on 18 July 2007.
4. In the case of two of the texts, Yve's and Graciela's, the second-hand citations were qualitatively somewhat different; they cited only the most recent source, the one it appeared they had consulted, but those sources attributed the propositions for which they had been cited to one or more earlier works.
5. As part of the effort to protect the privacy of the thesis writers, personal details are not given about them here. Following on a flip of a coin, the SS2 writer will be referred to as 'he' and the H2 writer as 'she'.

5

'My position, it is impossible': The writers' perspectives

So far it has been seen that the student writers were not fully successful in the important area of using sources effectively and appropriately, and that their work contained intertextual relationships which could be called plagiarism. This chapter will present the perspectives of the writers themselves. Nine of the writers—those at the master's level—were interviewed, and the discussion in this chapter draws heavily on those interviews. To the extent that there were similarities between the two groups in how they used sources, it is reasonable to think that many of the factors identified here apply to the writers at the PhD level as well.

Was It Intentional?

Chapter 3 examined the aspects of the student texts which could be called textual plagiarism. Was it also prototypical plagiarism? That is, did the writers intend to deceive about the relationship between their texts and their sources? Intention is difficult to get at; only the writers can provide direct evidence as to whether they intended to deceive, but when plagiarism (or any other proscribed act) is involved, denials of intention are often sceptically received. An account that is accepted as sincere can nonetheless be distorted by faulty recollection, imperfect awareness of motivations, etc. Thus the best evidence for the writers' intentions is (here and in any case when plagiarism has been alleged) circumstantial. In this section I will argue that the available circumstantial evidence suggests strongly that the writers did not intend to cheat.

The first piece of evidence is the writers' demeanour: in different ways they demonstrated that they were committed to their academic work and discussed questions related to their research with ease, enthusiasm and engagement[1]. Graciela, for example, had left a job in her country and come to Britain to do a master's degree in an area that was in no way related to her work, but in which she had a great deal of interest, saying 'I choose to come because I wanted to do this course, it was not required for [my employer]. This is something personal, really personal'[2].

Roula, on the other hand, saw connections between her degree and a later job. She had an interest in translation and at the time of our interviews was planning to become a translator. Her thesis work on metaphor in translation was, therefore, relevant for her future career. Helen also saw her research on textbooks for young learners as useful for the work she planned to do when she returned to Taiwan, teaching English to children. After one of our interviews she asked about my daughter, who was growing up in a multilingual environment, and as we chatted for a few moments, showed a genuine interest in children as language learners.

Maria's enthusiasm was not limited to her topic but extended to the experience of studying at a British university. Maria had done her BA in the UK before starting her master's course, and spoke passionately about the frustration she had felt as a student in Greece, which was the reason she had come to the UK for her undergraduate work. She described the pressures of a composition class in secondary school that was intended to prepare students to meet the university entry requirement of writing a long essay. An ambitious student, Maria tried, but the bar was set too high:

> Your level had to be very intellectual, very academic. . . . it was very difficult. For me it was pointless. You can't expect a sixteen-year-old to speak like a lecturer. . . . I never managed to reach that

level, I could never speak like a professor, I was only 16. . . . It's not possible in just one year to become absolutely fluent and absolutely intellectual. . . . So I could reach, say . . . the standard was twenty, the grades I used to get were seventeen or sixteen. It was not good, it was not enough. You could not enter the university with seventeen or sixteen. You needed a nineteen.

Maria described the strategy students used to meet these demands:

What most of my classmates used to do was memorize chapters or paragraphs of people that were very intellectual and they used to put these whole paragraphs in the composition they were writing so the teacher had the idea that, 'Oh, this student is very good', he's learning, but it was not like that, he was copying.

The result was a situation that Maria had found extremely alienating:

Yeah, but they were . . . imagine the classroom was 30–35 pupils, 20 of them were cheating, five of them were extremely intellectual and they were doing well, and the rest of them, including myself, we were just trying to cope with the situation. We were not intellectual, we did not want to cheat, so we were just trying to do our best.

However, Maria's best was not good enough to compete against the handful of brilliant students and the large group she perceived as cheaters, who achieved the place at university that Maria could not. As a result of this experience, Maria said she felt she could never sit another exam in Greece, and would not return to Greece to work when she finished her master's degree.

Given that her experiences of academic writing had been so frustrating in Greece, I asked her if work on her thesis had also been stressful. It had not, she said, because she was interested in the topic: 'I've chosen a topic, I wasn't given one, and it's my own research, so I enjoy doing it'. In addition to a strong degree of personal investment in her thesis topic, Maria had an extremely positive attitude towards university studies in Britain:

In Britain, it was so amazing the first time I sat an examination in England, we were given the exam sheets and the professor left the room and no one in the classroom just looked at the other table trying to copy. No one. Just everyone was just focused. In Greece people would start thinking like you know, what is the purpose of doing it, he left the classroom, now I can copy, the people would take the book out of the bag and he would start copying, or he would be you know helping a friend or something or turning around or he would shout or you know, it's the way we think. British people wouldn't do that. They trust you, and I think that's a good thing, because this makes you responsible. They trust you when they issue the paper and they leave you alone and this means that you are professional enough and responsible enough to sit down and write the exam. And, I mean, you have an amount of the responsibility. In Greece that would be absolutely . . . very naive.

Clearly Maria's contention that British students 'wouldn't do that', would not cheat, is assailable. What her account shows, though, is a deep appreciation for a learning context which she perceived could function on the basis of trust and personal responsibility. She contrasted that to her earlier experiences with a system that made cheaters of students by placing impossible (and unpedagogical) demands upon them. The relief she expressed at finding herself working within a system characterized by trust and responsibility— as she saw it—makes it difficult to believe that she was trying to defraud the system.

Maria and the other eight writers who were interviewed were fully engaged in and committed to their academic work. That does not, of course, make it impossible for one or more of them to have engaged in plagiarism deliberately, but it does make it less likely, something which must be weighed up together with the other available evidence about their intentions. Deceptive plagiarism is often understood as an effort to gain credit while avoiding work, but these writers are not a good fit for that picture either. Although the cumulative effect of repetition from sources was considerable, each writer used a range of different sources, and (as Currie, 1998, noted about the writer she studied) the time and energy expended on finding suitable passages and joining them together must have been considerable. When the process included modifying the source passage, the task was even more laborious.

52a For centuries evaluation has been used by classroom teachers as an equivalent of 'testing'.

[Kwan]

52b For centuries the term *evaluation* has been used by classroom teachers, who thought of it only in relation to the grading of students. For most educators, indeed, the idea of evaluation was essentially equivalent to the idea of testing.

[Popham, 1988, p. 1]

53a This is particularly so when the subjects want to protect themselves, to please the researcher, or even to show what they think are acceptable forms of behaviour.

[SS2]

53b This is especially true if the self-interests of the respondents appear to be attacked, or if they feel the need to protect themselves, to please the research worker, or to conform to what they consider are socially acceptable forms of behaviour.

[Lovell and Lawson, 1970, p. 86]

If the intention of these writers had been to copy from the sources to save time and energy, it seems unlikely that they would then have taken the trouble to make alterations of the sort seen in (52), (53), and the examples in Chapter 4. This again is not conclusive proof against deceptive plagiarism, but it is one more factor to be taken into account.

Another is the attitude towards plagiarism that the students themselves expressed. I was careful not to be the first to use the word 'plagiarism' in the interviews, but the students introduced it themselves, discussing it in terms that showed they were generally aware of the issue and concerned about avoiding plagiarism. At the end of our first interview Erden raised the issue as a subject he was concerned about, and identified what he saw as areas of difficulty, such as knowing whether a word is a commonly accepted term or 'some people's expressions', which would need to be cited. Other writers felt they had a clearer sense of what plagiarism was and was not. Maria said she had taken a study skills class that had been 'very helpful' and had taught her 'what plagiarism was about', and Ingrid had received a handout from her department. Roula reported several comments from her supervisor; one of them was that quotations should always include the year of publication and page number, otherwise 'the examiner is going to wonder you did the plagiarism'. The fact that the writers felt comfortable introducing plagiarism into our conversation suggests that they were not simultaneously and deliberately perpetrating the act.

Their openness extended beyond discussing plagiarism to other aspects of their source use. The nine writers who were interviewed were voluntary participants in a study that they knew would draw attention to their writing, and would involve their supervisors as well. All of the sources which were gathered for comparison were identified in some way by the writers (a point that holds true for the PhD students as well), either in the reference list or (in the case of some of the master's students) directly to me in a personal communication. Kwan, for example, had not included a reference list with her writing sample (which reached me in draft form) but when she realized it would be useful, she typed one up and sent it. Erden realized during our second interview that many of his sources had not yet been published and offered to lend me a number of articles. Yves' references too included materials which would have been difficult to obtain. He had given his supervisor his own copies, but suggested I contact the supervisor for access to them. The writers' openness about their sources (in spite of the fact that they did not always manage to identify them transparently in their texts) is yet another argument against the opaque source use having been due to deliberate deception.

Three writers (one of the master's students and two of the PhD students) carried that openness to an extreme by copying from their own supervisors' published works. It is not reasonable to think that those individuals were aware that copying of that nature could constitute plagiarism (e.g. a 48-word passage copied verbatim) and yet did it in the awareness that the one person best equipped to identify the copying was also the person who would read their text most closely. This and other indications about the writers make intentional deception a poor fit; other explanations for the textual plagiarism must therefore be sought.

Where Did It Come from?

If the textual plagiarism was not caused by the intention to deceive, where did it come from? A number of explanations emerge from the interviews with the student writers, supported by the analysis of the student texts and the existing literature. This section provides an (by no means exhaustive) examination of the causes of textual plagiarism.

Patchwriting as a Strategy

Paraphrase is a new way of expressing ideas which are attributable to a source, an independent rewording. The strategy of condensing, substituting synonyms and reordering that was found in many of the writing samples is not paraphrase; it is patchwriting (Howard, 1995, 1999). For the writers in this study, though, patchwriting was a third way, an alternative to quoting and paraphrasing which avoided the problems the writers associated with each. Excessive quotation was undesirable; as Helen said (and others echoed), it is 'better not to quote too much' (and Errey, 2002, reported a student who believed that too much quotation amounted to plagiarism). Indeed, in the hard fields explicitly marked quotation is quite unconventional so it was not a viable option at all for half of the writers.

Paraphrasing, however, carries two risks of its own. These writers were keenly aware there was a risk that nuances might be lost or that meaning might be distorted. Roula said, 'sometimes when you paraphrase something, you just miss the point of the book'. Kwan echoed Roula (and writers from other studies, e.g. Angélil-Carter, 2000): 'however hard you try I think there is still something that's between what is written in the book and what is written by yourself'. Paraphrase also involves the risk that the finished product will be inferior in expression to the original. As Ingrid said, 'it's quite hard . . . because they actually written in the best way of doing it'. Interestingly, her supervisor recognized this sentiment, saying 'many people when they read a piece of text think, well I can't possibly improve that, it makes its point so very, very clearly, so who am I to modify it and change it?' This is not an abstract or unfounded risk; in (54) where Helen tried to vary the language of her source, the result was awkward and ungrammatical:

54a However, Fox (1979) criticized West's *General Service list* for this 'minimum adequate vocabularies' is unable to help learners to deal with authentic language.

[Helen]

54b Fox (1979) argues that 'minimum adequate vocabularies' might be adequate for productive purposes, but that they leave learners seriously under-equipped to deal with authentic language.

[Nunan, 1995, p. 118]

For these writers, a paraphrase was not an attractive option: both the content and the form of expression were likely to suffer. In this light, Helen's changes in Example (55) can be interpreted as an effort to move away from the source, but to remain within her comfort zone—like the ice skater who takes her hand off the safety railing but remains within grabbing distance of it.

55a Nunan (1995:119) states that Richards' article is important in that it suggests different learners may need differentiated vocabulary lists, and the vocabulary lists should reflect learners' communicative needs.

[Helen]

55b Richards' article is an important one, suggesting as it does that we may need differentiated vocabulary lists for different learners, and that the lists should reflect the communicative needs of the learners.

[Nunan, 1995, p. 119]

Patchwriting as a Form of Paraphrase

The writers' comments also suggest that they conceived of paraphrase not as the process of finding an independent formulation to transmit the ideas in a source, but as a process of editing the source and changing its language. During our second interviews I asked them to identify quotations and paraphrased portions of their texts, and Helen identified the passage in (55a) as a paraphrase. When I asked her how she had gone about the process of paraphrasing (in the paragraph from which this extract is drawn), she said that she had the book open in front of her, and was looking at it as she wrote her own text. She added, 'really I didn't change a lot. Maybe passive to active and some words, I changed some words'.

Graciela discussed a similar case, in (56). This passage features one of her frequent strategies, combining explicitly signalled quotation with modified portions of the same source not marked as quotation. The changes in (56) were:

1. To add a citation, which became the subject of the sentence, replacing 'Most respondents'. This introduced a small distortion: while Maher and Best say that their *respondents* made these suggestions, in Graciela's version the authors now appear responsible for them.

2. Moving the phrases 'initial training' and 'in-service programmes' from their positions as headers for two sections, to replace the phrase 'under this heading'.

3. Replacing the phrase 'These included the following' with 'which include'.

4. Changing 'make' and 'increase' to 'making' and 'increasing', in line with change (3).

5. Adding the phrase 'From their research also emerges' to create a transition to the material from the second part of the source.

6. Omitting the source's reference to *qualifications*.

7 Replacing the phrase 'in pastoral care and related areas' with 'on this subject'.

8 Combining two references to respondents into a single reference.

56a Maher and Best (1985) <u>made some suggestions</u> to improve <u>initial training</u> and <u>in-service programmes</u>, which <u>include making pastoral care a compulsory component on all initial courses</u> and <u>increasing the length of the PGCE</u>. From their research also emerges <u>the need for more lecturers with specialist experience</u> on this subject. <u>As one respondent</u> in their study <u>pointed</u> out: <u>'Tutors on the PGCE should be trained in aspects of pastoral care: first train the trainers</u>!' (p. 65)

[Graciela]

56b Initial training

Most respondents <u>made some suggestions</u> under this heading. These <u>included</u> the following:

1 <u>make pastoral care a compulsory component on all initial courses</u>;

2 <u>increase the length of the PGCE</u> to make this possible;//

In-service programmes//

Teaching and researching

Several <u>respondents pointed</u> to <u>the need for more lecturers with specialist experience</u> and qualifications in pastoral care and related areas. <u>As one</u> put it: <u>'Tutors on the PGCE should be trained in aspects of pastoral care: first train the trainers</u>!'

[Maher and Best, 1985, pp. 64–65]

When she looked at this section of the text sometime after writing it, Graciela identified the words in quotation marks as quotation and everything else in the passage as paraphrase. She commented:

> Again, I used this paraphrase to summarize what the authors were saying. I did not refer to all their suggestions, but the ones I considered more relevant. I realise that I kept not only the main words but [some] parts of some sentences. The idea was, again, to put together what I thought were the main contributions of that section. I added the quotation because I thought it was an important idea and had a bit of humour.

Graciela's strategy, here and in other passages, was to quote directly where there was a purpose for it—one she had clearly reflected on—and to paraphrase elsewhere. Where she paraphrased, she retained the key words, 'in order' (as she explained about another passage), 'not to alter the meaning'. In this passage, though, she realized after the fact that more than the key words ('parts of some sentences') had been retained in the paragraph. Although Graciela clearly invested considerable effort in creating effective paraphrases, she too saw the task of paraphrasing as a process of changing the original.

Ingrid expressed this view more directly than any of the other respondents. When I asked her to explain the difference between quotation and paraphrase, she said:

> Quotation is just writing the exact what it already was, but a paraphrase is actually also saying what it was, but you just use . . . **changing it a little bit** so it won't be exactly what was said. It will have the same meaning.
>
> (emphasis added)

Among the portions of her text that Ingrid identified as paraphrased was (57). Her source, Ramsay et al., had been cited in the preceding sentence in the same paragraph:

57a By using <u>recombinant backcross lines containing short regions of donor chromosome introgressed into a constant recipient background QTLs</u> can <u>be located with</u> a <u>greater precision</u>.

[Ingrid]

57b The use of <u>recombinant backcross lines containing short regions of donor chromosome introgressed into a constant</u>

recipient background permits QTLs to be located with greater precision.
[Ramsay et al., 1996, p. 558]

Ingrid, it can be seen, had followed her own definition of paraphrasing: she changed Ramsay et al.'s sentence 'a little bit', substituting 'by using' for 'the use of', changing 'permits QTLs to be located' to 'QTLs can be located' and adding an indefinite article before 'greater precision'. Writers who understand paraphrasing to be an act of amending an original will inevitably produce new versions which are as close to the original as the last examples, and which may be too close for some readers. This was the view of Graciela's supervisor, who felt that in (56) the words 'making pastoral care a compulsory component on all initial courses' should have been placed in quotation marks.

Patchwriting to Find and Learn Academic Language

A paraphrasing strategy that sticks close to the language of the source offers a clear linguistic benefit: the chance to access phrases which are appropriate to the context and register.

58a This definition (by Bolam, 1986: 18), which is typical of many, in effect brings to the fore 'the emphasis of the in-service work on the improvement of the well-known triangular aspects of the human condition—knowledge, skills and attitudes' (Pyle and Sayers, 1980). But perhaps there is more to this than at first seems apparent.
[Kwan]

58b This definition (by Palmer, 1978) is typical of many, and in effect stresses the improvement of the well-known triangular aspects of the human condition—knowledge, skills and attitudes. But perhaps there is more to this than at first seems apparent.
[Pyle and Sayers, 1980, p. 10]

In (58) Kwan uses a definition which she correctly identifies as coming from Bolam, and follows it with a quotation which is correctly attributed to Pyle and Sayers (although the quotation itself is not accurate, containing as it does an addition Kwan has made). However, the definition that Pyle and Sayers were commenting on was not Bolam's. What Kwan has adopted from her source is a phraseological framework for presenting the definition she chooses to examine: *This definition (by [source]) is typical of many.*

It is interesting to note that in (58a) Kwan's 'brings to the fore' is a nicely academic-sounding chunk, and it is not present in the corresponding part of Pyle and Sayers. It is possible that she learned it from some other academic text and recycled it here. In a study of two writers at secondary level, Villalva (2006) found that one of them consciously reused chunks of language from sources in her own writing. However, copying was not a terminal stage; the chunks she copied became part of her lexicon. For that writer, copying was a successful learning strategy, and one that Roula's supervisor approved of:

> If you lift 'it is evident that the neglect of' into a totally different paper dealing with totally different matters, this is the everyday language of academic argument and negotiation. And published papers are a very good source of that because they've been through the gatekeepers, they've been revised, they've had their language tidied up. It's a very good model and it's what I recommend students do. 'Steal' the language. Don't steal the contents but steal the language. 'Distinguishes between x and y'. If they can write like that at the appropriate points, if they get it from looking through this and going for the language rather than the concepts and ideas.

Patchwriting is a process of altering and piecing together extracts from texts and as was seen in Chapter 4, the size of the text extracts and the alterations to them can vary. Ingrid created a quilt made up of large patches of a few different fabrics; other writers stitched together more and smaller patches to produce a more intricate design. At a certain point those patches look less like units in which an author might have a proprietorial interest and more like expressions which could be found in many contexts: *distinguishes x from y, brings to the fore, the second half of the eighth century.* Importantly, the fact that some of the longer copied chunks do *not* look like neutral, borrowable phrases to some experienced members of the academic discourse community does not preclude the possibility that the students may have thought of them that way.

As Ivanič notes,

> In order to become a member of a community, to take on its discourse, it is necessary to try it out in some way, and it is extremely hard to draw the lines between plagiarism, imitation and acquisition of a new discourse.
>
> (1998, p. 195)

The patchwriting in this study allowed the writers to try out the discourse of their new communities, giving them access to forms of expression which were appropriate to the academic texts they were writing. It is not possible to know, but is interesting to wonder, whether the writers gained some lasting benefit from this writing strategy, and through it were able to expand their linguistic repertoires.

'I'll Change It Later'

Aspects of the writers' processes also contributed to source-dependent language in the writing samples. Because of both the reluctance to paraphrase and time constraints, writers put material into drafts in a form close to the original, with the intention of trying to paraphrase it later. As Kwan explained,

> if possible, you know, when I finish all the writing and when I feel more confident about what I'm writing I might be able to adapt some of them [extracts from the source] into kind of paraphrasing, some of them, because, see, there might be a problem if you just quote all the time without paraphrasing the others, so I might be able to do that at the end, do the revision part.

Erden's comments on part of his text echo Kwan. I asked him to explain why he had chosen to cite a given work, and as he reviewed the citation, he became gradually aware of how similar his paraphrase was to the source, saying 'there are too much copied'. I pointed out that he had given a citation, although the passage was not in quotation marks, and asked if that made it okay. His answer was:

> No. You try to avoid this, but you know, when you are reading and taking a note, sometimes it is unavoidable. . . . for example, you couldn't remember it was exact copy or copying it one sentence or copying it his results, what they had done.

Roula had a similar moment of realization in our interview and concluded that when it was time to revise that part of her thesis, she would 'just try to change more the words'. However, this approach—write it down now and change it later—involves a real risk that the writers would not remember later which parts need to be revised. Time constraints would make a systematic approach of checking every reference against the original prohibitive, as Erden explained: 'to go through the whole notes and look at the sentence by sentence. . . . I cannot go directly that way because probably I am going to use hundreds of citations, hundreds of articles. . . . I mean, my position, it is impossible'.

Theory and Practice

Another factor which contributed to problematic source use was a gap between what the writers knew about source use and plagiarism in theory and practice. An explanation commonly offered for unintentional plagiarism is that students do not know enough about what it is. At a general level, the writers did not lack knowledge or information about what plagiarism is (although there were some misconceptions; Roula understood her supervisor to have said that leaving out the year of publication from a reference could look like plagiarism). A greater problem for the writers in this study, though, was a limited understanding of the practical implications of that knowledge.

During the first interviews students were asked to complete several tasks designed to indicate their knowledge about source use conventions (see the Appendix for details). The tasks were:

- to match six terms related to citations (quotation, reference/citation, paraphrase, quotation marks/inverted commas, source and reference list) with their definitions;
- to translate the same terms into the student's first language;
- to explain the difference between quoting and paraphrasing; and
- to identify a paraphrase and a quotation in an extract from a research article.

The students' performance on the tasks demonstrated a generally strong level of knowledge in these areas. Four of the students—Ingrid, Maria, Graciela and Roula—matched all the terms with their definitions correctly. Another four—Erden, Pierre, Kwan and Helen—reversed one set of terms each. The remaining student, Yves, matched three of the terms and definitions incorrectly. The fact that eight of the nine participants made either no errors or one error only suggests a reasonably good understanding of the terms and their meanings.

The translation, somewhat surprisingly, proved significantly harder than the matching of definitions. The purpose of the task was not to check the students' answers, but to observe how promptly and confidently they were able to answer, since hesitation or an inability to answer might reveal incomplete understanding of the term. Only three of the writers were able to translate the terms easily, while five provided translations but hesitated and expressed uncertainty over one or more of the words. However, in retrospect it seems that this difficulty was not so much a reflection of what they knew, but of the fact that their recent encounters with academic discourse had been in English. As Ingrid explained, 'I actually don't know what they are in Norwegian, the exact words . . . I haven't written Norwegian for so long'.

All of the students could explain the difference between a quotation and a paraphrase, and made two points consistently: that a quotation is enclosed in quotation marks, and that the wording of a paraphrase differs from that of the original. Not surprisingly then, each was able to identify a quotation and a paraphrase from a research article, presumably by using the approach that Graciela voiced: 'it's also in inverted commas, I mean, that's the way you identify a quotation, by the inverted commas', while sections which had a reference but not quotation marks were paraphrases.

However, when asked in the second interview to identify quotations and paraphrases in their own writing, the same writers found this less easy. There was hesitation; some passages which were traceable back to sources were left unmarked; others were marked as paraphrase when the language was identical to, or very similar to, that of the source. Several marked language as quotation although it was not inside quotation marks. Every student but Yves marked parts as paraphrase that appeared to be quotation. In short, the distinction between quotation and paraphrase, which the writers had found easy to articulate, became less clear when they attempted to apply it to their own writing. Similar findings have emerged from studies of US university students and lecturers (Roig, 1997, 2001); in those studies participants had difficulty identifying plagiarism and paraphrase in sample texts.

Similarly, Ingrid was comfortable relating what she knew about plagiarism, based on an information sheet from her department:

> It just said we're not supposed to do that [plagiarism] and that . . . you can probably write as much as you want that other people already written as long as you kind of give the references and don't pretend it's your own words. . . . you put in the quotation marks and have the reference there.

Yet Ingrid's writing contained 14 passages with over 90 per cent of the language in common with her sources, and no quotation marks.

The transition from principles to their practical application involved a degree of uncertainty. The categories which seemed easy to define—quotation, paraphrase, plagiarism—developed permeable boundaries in practice. Roula discussed the passage in (59) in our second interview. She had marked part of this passage as paraphrase (the sentence containing the reference to Cooper and possibly the next sentence as well; her markings are not entirely clear). The rest was not marked either as paraphrase or quotation.

> **59a** As a consequence of this another question arises<u>: If dead metaphors are not metaphors, what are they? One popular answer is idioms.</u> According to Cooper (1986: 123) <u>this could</u>

not be generally true in an everyday sense of 'idiom'. We could not, for example, ordinarily regard 'pig' as an idiomatic way of referring to gluttons or policemen. In an everyday sense, moreover, idiom and metaphor are not exclusive of one another. Some people would want to call 'buck up' both metaphorical and idiomatic. So it is not a good label for expressions which cannot be metaphors.

[Roula]

59b If dead metaphors are not metaphors, what are they? One popular answer is *idioms*[7]. But this could not be generally true in an everyday sense of 'idiom'. We would not, for example, ordinarily regard 'pig' as an *idiomatic* way of referring to gluttons or policemen (not like 'bobby'). In an everyday sense, moreover, idiom and metaphor are not exclusive of one another. Some people would want to call 'buck up' both metaphorical and idiomatic. So it is not, as familiarly used, a good label for expressions which, on the views being considered, cannot be metaphors.

[Cooper, 1986]

As we looked at the passage together, Roula began to feel that she had not changed a great deal in her paraphrase, and would change more in the next round of revisions. She commented, though: 'I thought it would be okay if I put it like that. Of course I mentioned that it's Cooper's words, so its not plagiarism but . . .' Roula had *not* mentioned that it was Cooper's words in the conventional way, by using quotation marks, but she believed she had, and that she had created something which was not fully appropriate source use but was not plagiarism either.

Deducing the Rules

In some ways the difficulties that the writers encountered in putting information about plagiarism and source use into practice resemble the difficulties that arise in trying to apply plagiarism policies to specific cases: principles and definitions which seem sound at a theoretical level may prove to be more complex in application. When faced with complexities, the writers tried to draw on the rules they (thought they) understood to deduce answers for specific situations. However, they were not always fully successful.

Erden distinguished between acceptable and unacceptable copying, saying 'people just copy the whole paragraph and use it' and said 'I am against this type of things'. Repeating shorter chunks was not a problem, though: 'copying a whole paragraph without giving citation, it is a plagiarism. But taking a note in one paper, just one sentence comes directly or, yeah, one or two sentence or one explanation, it is I think acceptable'. It seems unlikely that Erden had been informed by an official source (e.g. his supervisor, another lecturer, a writing guide) that copying two sentences is appropriate, and his 'I think' shows that this was Erden's interpretation, rather than a rule he had been presented with.

Ingrid, more than any of the other writers, was able to articulate rules that she had deduced. She was against secondary citation if she had no familiarity with the earlier source: 'when you're referring to someone's experiments you should refer to *their* experiments'. She said, therefore, that if she came across a reference to a potentially useful paper, she would try to read it, or 'at least parts of it so you can actually say that you know what that article was about'. That much at least appears to be a sound principle, but another of Ingrid's conclusions may not elicit universal agreement. Like Erden, she distinguished between appropriate and inappropriate copying, but for Ingrid the distinction was based on the part of the source which was used. Findings were sacrosanct, but the background elements found in the introduction to a research article were akin to common knowledge and therefore borrowable:

> Yeah, that's some kind of, yeah, you can get it from so many different . . . and also when you read, this is what I found, you read through all these articles and you find out that they actually write, they have quite similar introduction, the introduction are quite similar in all the different articles. So if you just read the introduction you actually really similar. And I just can't see whose words are theirs and I just . . . put them because that's kind of like

common knowledge that most people know, it's easy to find it, you can find it anywhere.

Like Erden, she thought that quantity mattered: 'as long as you don't copy, like, loads . . .' it was acceptable. Although Ingrid's writing sample provides abundant examples of problematic source use, it is possible to trace in it the effects of the rules the writer believed to apply to it. With the exception of the initial paragraph, all of her text can be traced back to a source, so cumulatively Ingrid did copy 'loads', but what she copied came from a number of different sources; she did not copy 'loads' from any one work.

Ingrid's writing sample contains 11 paragraphs; most of them were quite long (one more than a page in length). The first paragraph, apparently written by Ingrid, identifies the topic. Paragraph 2 identifies some of the characteristics of the genus of plants she was researching and contains no citations at all, although three sources can be shown to have been used. One of them, and the corresponding portion of Ingrid's text, is shown in (60). The passage from Kennard et al. (1994) is taken from the beginning of their introduction. Paragraph 3 gives an overview of quantitative trait locus analysis, the method used in the thesis, and is divided into four chunks taken from three sources, only one of which is cited. This paragraph, too, contains what could be classed as background information.

60a Brassica oleracea is an important vegetable crop species, which includes fully cross-fertile cultivars or form groups with widely different morphological characteristics, such as cabbage, broccoli, cauliflower, Brussels sprout and kohlrabi. Genetic studies has been limited because long generation time of the biennials, the complex inheritance patterns of some trait, and the difficulty in overcoming self-incompatibility.

[Ingrid]

60b Brassica oleracea is an important vegetable crop species which includes fully cross-fertile cultivars or form groups with widely-differing morphological characteristics (cabbage, broccoli, cauliflower, collards, Brussels sprouts, kohlrabi, and kale). Genetic studies of *B. oleracea* have been limited in part by the long generation time of the biennials, the complex inheritance

> patterns of some traits, and the difficulty in overcoming self-incompatibility.
>
> *[Kennard et al., 1994, p. 721]*

With paragraph 4, though, Ingrid begins to review findings of existing research on her topic. The 42-line-long paragraph begins with a citation to Kennard et al. (1994), and the rest of the paragraph comes, with only minor rewording, from that paper. Paragraph 5 begins with a generic-sounding statement (61a):

> **61a** <u>The control of flowering time is a process of primary importance in agriculture and also of great scientific interest for the understanding of plant development</u>.
>
> *[Ingrid 3:1a]*
>
> **61b** <u>The control of flowering time is a process of primary importance in agriculture and also of great scientific interest for the understanding of plant development.</u>
>
> *[Lagercrantz et al., 1996, p. 13]*

This sentence from Lagercrantz et al. (1996) comes from their introduction; that paper is cited later in Ingrid's text but not in proximity to this extract. The rest of the paragraph, though, reports the findings of Camargo and Osborn (1996), who are cited. In other words, wherever specific findings are reported, a citation appears, but where language from a source is used for generic statements about the background to the research, the citation is usually absent. This pattern continues throughout the text. Ingrid has followed the principles she explained: if you write about their findings, cite them. If you report their background information, do not.

Importantly, the rule that Ingrid had evolved was not that a citation was *unnecessary* for background information, but that it was preferable *not* to give a citation for background information. She discussed her process of deciding what to reference and what not:

> Yeah. So that's how I've tried, I don't know how I'm supposed to do it, but when I'm referring to their experiments I try to put them in, and when I just using the same background information that they probably got from someone else I don't use, putting

the names, **because I don't know where they got it from, and you're supposed to use the original source and since I don't know what the original source is I just put the article that I read.**

(emphasis added)

Keeping in mind Ingrid's earlier comment about introductions, that they are 'really similar' to each other, her conclusion is logical. Ingrid believed that other writers' introductions were similar to each other because they were working to her rule: borrowed language is fine provided it is background information. Therefore the background information in a given article introduction could have come from anywhere. Knowing that 'you're supposed to use the original source', Ingrid could *not* give a citation for some sorts of material because the original source could not be identified!

Other Balls in the Air

Although not a topic raised directly by the students in our interviews, it is likely that another factor contributing to the presence of textual plagiarism may have been the degree of importance they accorded it among their other priorities. Plagiarism can easily become a larger-than-life issue, given its consequences and its special status as an academic crime, but these writers had other balls in the air; while they were concerned about avoiding plagiarism and about using sources appropriately, that was not their sole objective. The substantial independent research projects they were engaged in were exercises in multi-tasking. There were data to be collected, methods to decide on, questionnaires to write or plants to grow or people to interview or texts to analyse. There was a great deal to read and a thesis to write—in a second language. Some had coursework still to complete, and some had aspirations of having a private life as well. The writers did not consider source use to be a matter of low priority, but it could not be their single concern. If they took their eyes off the ball from time to time, it is not surprising.

In summary, the textual plagiarism in the student writing came about as a result of a variety of causes and contributing factors related to what the students knew, believed and were learning to do. Helen's explanation of her source use touched upon a number of the themes in this section.

Her comments related to the passage that appears in (62a), the eighth item in a list.

62a 8. To investigate whether the activities and exercises help learners to extend and develop their vocabulary in a purposeful and structural way (Cunningsworth, 1995: 39).

[Helen 5:1b]

62b It is worth examining the nature of the activities and exercises to ensure that they help learners to extend and develop their vocabulary in a purposeful and structured way.

[Cunningsworth, 1995, p. 39]

When I asked her whether the passage in her text was a quotation, she answered

> I think paraphrase . . . But I used a lot of his words, so I put a page number. It's not really a quotation, just the vocabulary she used, I think very near to my ideas so I used his words.

Helen's answer contains several interesting points. First, I understood Helen's 'I think' not to be simply a hedge but to be literally true; she thought she had paraphrased, but was not sure. Secondly, her source use has a hybrid quality: 'I used his words' but 'It's not really a quotation'. Third, Helen gave a page number because she had 'used a lot of his words'; she made an effort to signal how she had used the source, although many readers may not understand the signal. Finally, Helen believes that how she references the passage should be determined by the nature of the content she reports. The author's ideas were 'very near to my ideas' so by repeating the language Helen was not appropriating the author's ideas, 'just the vocabulary'.

Helen, like the other writers who agreed to take part in this study, was a determined and ambitious student who cared about getting things right, but did not always succeed. Given that the writers were students, it is only to be expected that they would not always get it right. It was important, though, that they should have the chance to learn and improve.

How Did They Learn?

How did the writers learn about what they were supposed to do with their sources? In our interviews they identified several sources of learning, some of which had been more influential than others. Experience with writing, particularly in academic contexts, was an area included in our first interviews. Roula and Maria had attended British universities for their BAs, and had done writing assignments as part of their coursework. Graciela had studied journalism as an undergraduate and understandably wrote a great deal on that course. Erden had worked in a research establishment before beginning his master's degree and had prior experience with research writing. The other writers, though, had had considerably less experience with writing in academic contexts. Yves and Pierre, the engineering students, in particular said that they had written very little as part of their undergraduate education. In that respect they were not unusual; there is considerable evidence that students outside the English-speaking world do less writing than British and American university students (Dong, 1998; Gosden, 1996, p. 114; Timm, 2007; Ventola, 1992, p. 193), and indication that limited experience has a negative impact on their ability to do academic writing in English (Gosden, 1996, p. 116).

The students in the social sciences and humanities had done several extended writing assignments as part of their master's courses before beginning their theses. The engineers, by contrast, not only had done little other writing, they did not submit any portion of their theses in draft form before handing in the final version.

Another route for learning was seen above: writing their theses required the students to read in their subject area, and as they read works produced by more experienced members of their discourse communities, they deduced how sources were used. In other words, the published sources they used served as their models.

The supervisor was also a significant figure. As Roula said, discussing her decisions about how to reference, 'the tutor has to play a part of this, he has to be a part of the whole thing, to read the paraphrases and quotations and tell you if you're doing the right place, or if you have to rewrite it, or if you don't have to just mention it at all'. In her reasonable desire to be guided by her supervisor, Roula apparently was not aware of how much of her source use was not visible to her supervisor. All of the nine students had received comments on their writing samples from their supervisors, but Roula was one of the few who had received comments specifically about source use. Those comments tended to be about the visible aspects of citation, such as which sources to cite. Helen, for example, said that her supervisor had advised her to consult a specific journal to find other work related to her topic. However, there was no indication in any of the interviews that the supervisors had discussed with their students the instances of opaque source use that were documented in Chapter 3, since, until our interviews, the supervisors had (quite naturally) not compared the student texts to their sources.

Ingrid highlighted the problematic consequence of the lack of feedback: she said that since no one told her she was using sources the wrong way, she assumed that what she was doing was acceptable. Ingrid also, as noted above, made questionable assumptions about how published authors in her field write, and made her referencing fit those assumptions. The same factor lies behind both these problems: occlusion. Ingrid did not get feedback from her supervisor about her source use because the real relationship between her text and her sources was not visible to him. Similarly, Ingrid's efforts to deduce how published writers had used sources were unlikely to succeed, because she could not see their processes, only the finished product. As a result, although she—and the other writers—had important lessons they needed to learn about using sources, good opportunities for doing so passed them by.

This chapter has identified a number of the causes of textual plagiarism in the writing samples. I have argued that the students did not repeat language from their sources in an attempt to cheat, but that they did what can best be called patchwriting, and that it came about for a variety of reasons connected to their learning, their writing processes and their ability to put declarative knowledge about how—and how not—to use sources into practice.

Chapter 4 pointed to the problem that textual plagiarism was common in the student corpus. A greater problem still can now be identified: that the writers had not learned, and were unlikely to learn, that their source use was not only unacceptable, but was unacceptable in ways which could get them into trouble.

Notes

1 None of the writers was known to me before they responded to my call for research participants. My impressions of their engagement in their work arise exclusively from the contact I had with them during the research process.
2 Non-standard lexical and grammatical features in the text examples and interviews are preserved.

6

The readers

How did the readers respond to the students' texts? The readers whose reactions are most accessible are the supervisors of the nine master's students, since they took part in interviews. In addition, since all eight PhD theses had passed, and the students had been awarded degrees on the basis of them, it can be inferred that neither the supervisors nor the examiners had strong criticisms to make of the way sources were used (nor of any other aspect of the theses). However, it emerged from the interviews with the supervisors of the master's students that they did not have a clear picture of their students' source use before our interviews. Thus, it cannot be concluded that the supervisors and examiners of the PhD theses approved of the source use in those texts; it seems more likely that they too were not aware of features they may well have objected to.

The supervisors' responses to the writing samples are valuable not only because they reveal individual perceptions of what is desirable and appropriate in student writing at that level, but also because, as representatives of their academic disciplines, and in their roles as gatekeepers, the supervisors read their students' work with an eye to what is likely to be considered appropriate by other members of their disciplines. Their comments answer four broad questions: (1) How did the supervisors evaluate the visible aspects of their students' source use within the context of their research projects? (2) How did they react to the opaque source use? (3) What are the prospects for detecting inappropriate source use? (4) Did individual supervisors respond similarly or differently to their students' source use?

Reactions to the Source Use in Context

At the time of the interviews, the supervisors of the nine master's students had read the writing samples and given their students some feedback on them. Because of differences in the writing context (e.g. departmental procedures) and the students' working processes, the supervisors had engaged with the texts in various ways. For example, Maria had already completed one draft of the text we worked with, given it to her supervisor, received feedback on it, revised it, and received feedback on the new version before I interviewed her supervisor. Yves and Pierre, by contrast, showed their supervisor no preliminary drafts of their theses before handing in the final version for examination, so he had read them only in their final form, and not while they were under development.

I began each interview by asking the supervisors to comment on the writing samples generally, and on how their use of sources contributed to the larger text. Their responses quite naturally varied. Jenny Cain supervised both Graciela and Maria, and had this to say about Graciela's work:

> I thought on the whole that she was doing a very good job. She was quite, I think she was quite insecure about what she'd written, and I felt able to reassure her that she was very much on the right track. And I'd written a few pages or at least a page of comments and I think I went through that and expanded on the points that I'd made, like possibly restructuring things slightly, and adding cues and maps and things to help the reader navigate the text.

She was less enthusiastic about Maria's writing sample, but recognized it as an improvement on an earlier draft: 'I'm happier, although I'm still not convinced that it's quite where it should be . . . but I thought it was vastly improved, I'd say that much'.

Ingrid's supervisor, John Frost, was guardedly positive about her coverage of the relevant research literature, saying 'she's certainly got a lot of relevant papers. She hasn't got very many, she's got a dozen here and she could have found thirty, forty . . . but clearly she's found a lot of key ones'. His qualified approval was accompanied by an explanatory note:

> Ingrid came from an animal background rather than a plant background and I think she was probably more interested in humans, so the problems of working with plants are something which are quite new for her and create special problems, not only in terms of knowledge and what you can and can't do, but I think given that she started from a rather different sort of background, she's made a reasonable job of trying to understand what people are doing and why they're trying to do it.

Dr. Brown, who supervised Erden's thesis, said that the writing sample was fairly thorough and comprehensive. I wouldn't be recommending . . . I wouldn't be suggesting to him he's missed anything relevant out particularly. No, it's fairly concise. I mean, the introduction maybe to start with is actually a bit too broad, but then given that he's fairly concise it doesn't matter too much, so no problems.

As these comments indicate, although the supervisors could identify points for improvement, their evaluations of the writing samples were on balance more positive than negative. At this stage no supervisor said directly or implied that there were flaws so serious that that writer was at risk of not finishing, or of failing. On the basis of the features that could be observed simply by reading them, the writing samples were acceptable.

Reactions to Opaque Source Use

The reactions changed, though, when we looked at extracts from the writing samples together with the sources the students had used. After looking at the first passage from Ingrid's sample, Dr Frost said:

> That is not what they're expected to do, and if I'd spotted it I would have been very concerned about it, yes. If they're going to do that

sort of thing then they should put it straight in quotation marks, say this is taken from so on and so on, yeah.

Later, having looked at other examples, he said that if similar source use occurred in the final draft, the dissertation would be likely to fail. He also labelled it plagiarism, although indirectly:

> The rules quite clearly state that straight copying is plagiarism, so plagiarism shouldn't be, is not tolerated, so she's certainly breaking the rules very clearly . . . [*reading aloud*] 'if you wish to transcribe another person's, word for word another person's writing, this should be in the form . . .' the implication is that not to have quoted is plagiarism.

The early reaction of Erden's supervisor was similar; he said, 'I would be concerned if there were quite a few paragraphs like that throughout the thesis which I could specifically identify as being word to word from somewhere else, then I would be objecting'.

Dr Morse was supervisor to two participants in the study and was more critical of Kwan than of Helen. Commenting on the passage in Kwan's work which appeared as (58) in Chapter 5, he said 'Oh, well, that's a mess. That would have to be redone. I mean, that's all over the place, isn't it really?' Of Helen's text in (63), though, he said, 'so *this* sort of lifting, plagiarism, I wouldn't say, again, especially since she has got the quote and the page number, I wouldn't get terribly upset about. I mean, [it] wouldn't fail the dissertation. But it would bring it down a bit'.

63a In addition to gap-filling, there should be a variety of techniques to practise new words, such as word class change, crossword completion, crossword creation, multiple choice, sentence creation from a table, etc. (Williams and Dallas, 1984: 205).

[Helen]

63b Each unit of the workbook also contains a 'Using New Words' Section, employing a variety of techniques in addition to gap-filling, such as word class change, crossword completion, crossword creation, multiple choice, sentence creation from a table, etc.

[Williams and Dallas, 1984, p. 205]

The same words, 'mess' and 'lifting', arose in Jenny Cain's discussion of part of Maria's writing sample, but she was less direct in criticizing Graciela's work:

> There's a continuum from the pedantics of getting the punctuation right to sort of outright plagiarism, and to me, the sort of mistakes she's making are toward the very small end, and I think the spirit of the mistakes that she's making is that they're kind of small scale, but I think it's worth drawing her attention to them, because I think she'd be chagrined to find that she was doing this.

It is interesting that the supervisors both introduced the idea of plagiarism and backed away from it. The statement, above, that what Graciela had done was not plagiarism, was the first time the word had been used in our interview. Our discussion up to that point had established the presence of infelicities in Graciela's writing, but there had been nothing in my questions to suggest the ethical impropriety that the word connotes, and quite a bit in Cain's responses to indicate that she thought innocuous explanations could be found. By disclaiming plagiarism as a fitting description for what Graciela had done, she simultaneously acknowledged that it was not an unthinkable description.

Morse gave a similarly ambivalent answer. He too 'wouldn't say' that Helen's work constituted plagiarism, but again, his was the first mention of plagiarism in our interview. Calling what Helen did 'lifting' (as Maria's supervisor did) was an interesting choice of words, since 'lifting' is a euphemism for 'stealing'. He was only slightly more direct in discussing Kwan's text, saying 'I think probably a lot of what you've highlighted there, colleagues would regard as minor plagiarism'. He thus avoided committing himself to the view that it was plagiarism while not dismissing the possibility entirely.

While looking at Yves' writing, Dr Vane brought up a past case of plagiarism involving a student in his department. I asked him if he saw a connection between that case and Yves' work. His answer appeared to be 'no', but it was indirect and ambiguous: 'It is not serious, I would say. He does refer to a reference in there, but in a loose way, and there are substantial bits of that report which are his'. Neither Erden's supervisor nor Roula's mentioned plagiarism while we were speaking about the writing samples, but both did so when the discussion had taken a more general turn. Although they did not apply the term to the writing we looked at, the fact that they introduced the topic indicates that they saw it as not irrelevant to our discussion.

Interestingly, even though Ingrid's supervisor was quite vehement in his objections to Ingrid's source use, and appeared (as quoted above) to call it plagiarism, he did so indirectly. Ingrid was 'breaking the rules very clearly' and after reading the rules aloud he concluded that 'the *implication* is that not to have quoted is plagiarism' (emphasis added).

This ambivalence on the part of the supervisors may indicate a belief that different views were possible. As Morse said, his 'colleagues would regard as minor plagiarism' something that he was not prepared to label with that word, and Cain thought 'there is some interpretation involved. I think some people might be much stricter, others might be more lenient still'. Plagiarism, therefore, was a judgement call, and the way the supervisors discussed their students' writing suggests that one reason for their reluctance to commit themselves to a judgement was that they were taking contextual factors into account in addition to what they could see in the student texts. Quantity and especially location appeared to be important considerations for Brown in considering Erden's work. After looking at the first paragraph of Erden's writing sample, and its source, he said:

> I would be concerned if there were quite a few paragraphs like that throughout the thesis which I could specifically identify as being word to word from somewhere else, then I would be objecting . . . I would let it go in this particular case because clearly it is not happening further on.

We looked at four other passages, and then I asked him to comment on (64).

64a Faure et al., (1998) determined that in-vitro shoot Organogenesis of peppermint and spearmint was obtained from leaf discs. Best result were obtained when explants were cultured for two weeks onto MS medium supplementing with 300 mm mannitol, 2.0 mm BA and 2.0 mm IBA and then transferred on a medium without mannitol and containing 0.5 mm NAA. 9.0 mm BA and 0.5 mm TDZ. They achieved 78% regeneration for peppermint and 49% spearmint.

[Erden]

64b *In vitro* shoot organogenis of peppermint and spearmint was obtained from leaf disks. . . . Best results were obtained when explants were cultured for two weeks onto Murashige and Skoog medium supplemented with 300 mM mannitol, 2.0 µM 6-benzyladenine and 2.0 µM indole-3-butyric acid, and then transferred on a medium without mannitol and containing 0.5 µM α-naphthaleneacetic acid, 9.0 µM 6-benzyladenine and 0.5 µM thidiazuron. Using these culture conditions, percentages of regeneration were 78% for peppermint and 49% for spearmint.

[Faure et al., 1998, p. 209]

He said:

> Well, it's this difficulty you see, this literature review, when he's got to this point he is just telling us what individual, what other people have done quite specifically and again, I mean, coming up where it is, I think you would overlook it. If it was to come up in the discussion it would be an entirely different matter. Certainly three or four examples like that you would not expect in the discussion.

In this response there is tacit acknowledgement that the source use is not ideal (or else there would be nothing to 'overlook'), along with a reason not to consider it a serious flaw (it appears in the literature review and not in the discussion of the findings).

In this response Brown also suggests a reason for the repeated language: Erden's task in that portion of his text is essentially repetitive, 'just telling us . . . what other people have done'. Other supervisors also identified possible explanations for source-dependent writing other than intentional deception. Dr Vane was prepared to accept certain deviations from citation conventions in Pierre and Yves' work because of previous experience with French students: 'a problem we have with the French students is that they come to us with a French style of writing and presenting reports and it usually takes them a little while to get used to things, and we accept that'. He, along with others, also believed that the fact that the writers were NNSEs was a possible cause of source use problems.

HV: We have people who have great difficulty in expressing things in their own way. I guess this is to do with language. And I suspect the easiest way out is to see how other people have used ideas, and I don't think we ... we're not happy that they're quoting other people's work, effectively that's what they're doing, and we don't encourage it, we like them to write it in their own words, but when it comes to overseas students there is a problem.

DP: Particularly overseas students?

HV: Yeah. We find that most of the home-based students are able to express ideas. There are instances where they have difficulties. But one notices this in overseas students more.

Dr Morse echoed that idea in reference to (65).

65a In teaching non-native speakers, teachers might introduce new vocabulary which learners already know its cultural and linguistic background knowledge (Taylor, 1990: 6).

[Helen]

65b In teaching non-native speakers, then, we might introduce new vocabulary into the context of what our learners already know, culturally as well as linguistically.

[Taylor, 1990, p. 6]

Here Helen has included some chunks of language from her source and tried to modify the source in other places. She does this cautiously at first by deleting 'then' and substituting 'teachers' for 'we'. When she tries more substantive changes at the end, though, the result is syntactically flawed. Morse commented,

I'm sure that's one of the major problems that non-native speakers have. It must be, it must be so difficult for them to write; to read, and then write in their own words. I mean, it's a highly skilled operation, paraphrase. . . . And she's trying to paraphrase. And she probably feels she's given a quote already . . . and she didn't want to give another quote, because it might seem like she's quoting all the time, and not writing.

The fact that they could find other explanations for source use problems may have helped the supervisors to discount the possibility that it was deceptive plagiarism. In addition, the supervisors took what they knew about the students personally into consideration. Dr Brown believed that he might not judge another writer as benevolently as he judged Erden: 'what we've talked about I think would influence me in perhaps other circumstances without knowing the student'. Personal considerations factored into Jenny Cain's view of Maria's and Graciela's source use as well:

> I certainly don't see any will to plagiarize or circumvent conventions wilfully. Probably not in either of them. I think probably in Maria's case, she's quite young, and this is terrible, it sounds like I'm criticizing them personally or something, I hope it doesn't come across that way, but I think that she probably doesn't realize the seriousness of using things in this way. I certainly don't think, I don't think that's she's thinking that she's doing something wrong and is going to get away with it, I don't think that's an issue at all, I think it's just, as I say, a lack of awareness of how serious these things can be. So I would certainly put it down to that, I don't think that there's any attempt to plagiarize.

Neither writer intended to plagiarize 'wilfully', so other explanations were needed: Maria was 'quite young' and 'probably [didn't] realize the seriousness' of the way she had used sources. Graciela, as noted above, would 'be chagrined to find that she was doing this', so her source use problems were the result of an oversight, not intentional deception.

The theme of lack of knowledge or understanding, present in Cain's discussion of Maria's work, arose in other explanations from the supervisors. Morse believed that, because Helen had identified her sources throughout the text, there was no attempt at concealment. He commented, 'I think one would have to talk to her and see if she just didn't understand the conventions'. Later he tried to find a pattern in Helen's use of quotation marks which might reveal a misunderstanding about source use.

66a Broughton et al (1978: 172) suggest a criterion for topic selection that '<u>whatever is a natural topic in the mother tongue is a suitable topic for English</u>.'

[Helen]

66b <u>Whatever is a natural topic in the mother tongue is a suitable topic for English</u>.

[Broughton et al., 1978]

Morse pointed out that (66a) begins with the name of the author and a reporting verb, and speculates that

> EM: Maybe she just feels that when you use that form 'he says that' that what comes thereafter is expected to be a quote. I just don't know. But that would be a hypothesis. It's either, either she's aware of it and then that triggers, 'oh, I'd better put quotation marks in'. But when she's integrating the text, she's still aware that it's taken from the text, but it just doesn't trigger enough sensitivity to think, 'oh I'd better put quotation marks in there' and you know it's just a genuine error. Or she feels that is highlighted because she's . . . gone on to put a quote in, whereas the others aren't highlighted and I won't be so aware that they are quotes, as indeed I wasn't.
> DP: That second hypothesis is that it's . . .
> EM: . . . is that it's deliberate, yeah. And I'd tend to go for the first, I think . . . knowing Helen . . . I'd tend to go for the first.

In this extract, Morse weighs up two competing explanations. The first is that using a reporting verb 'triggers' Helen to think 'oh, I'd better put quotation marks in'. The second is that she thinks she does not need quotation marks when she does *not* use a reporting verb, because in those cases her *de facto* quotation is not 'highlighted' and Morse will not 'be so aware that they are quotes, as indeed [he] wasn't'. The second of these leaves open the possibility of deceptive intent: if her supervisor is not aware of how she uses sources, Helen might be able to get away with something inappropriate. Again the writer's personal credibility is a factor as well: 'knowing Helen', Morse discounts the latter possibility.

Two points in the way the supervisors assessed the writers' intentions are noteworthy. First, those that took a position at all believed that intentional deception was not the cause of the source use problems in the writing samples. Even Dr Frost, who was quite unhappy with Ingrid's source use, did not commit himself to intentional deception as a cause. When I asked him whether he thought that could be the explanation, he said 'I don't know whether I'm in a position to comment on that'. Later, though, he said: 'I'm quite confident that it is very, very common', suggesting that Ingrid did not set out to cheat—unless he believed that cheating is 'very, very common'. The conclusion that was reached in Chapter 4, that the problems with source use in the writing samples were not instances of prototypical plagiarism, is therefore one that the supervisors tended to support.

Secondly, the supervisors hesitated to pass judgement on the source use in the writing samples, and needed to take contextual factors, particularly those that spoke to intention, into account. This highlights the fact that plagiarism in its prototypical form is an intentional act of wrongdoing. If the element of intent is not present, then plagiarism—regardless of the extent of the borrowing—is a very strong word, and a contestable one. It was seen in Chapter 1 that cases of alleged plagiarism are seen very differently by different people, and that a single writer's practices can attract responses ranging from 'sloppy' to 'dirty'. Part of the difficulty in reaching a consensus about a specific case of plagiarism may be due to the tendency to look outside the text to understand what has happened. People who know an accused individual as a (hitherto) respected colleague (or student, or author) will be inclined to see the putative plagiarism as having some other explanation than dishonesty, while those who either lack personal knowledge of the writer, or wish to conclude that plagiarism has occurred, can do so by focusing on the texts.

The importance of intention—and the difficulty of judging it without access to information about the writer, as well as the text—means that even though the supervisors did not charge their students with deceptive plagiarism, the students were not safe from such an accusation from someone else. The simple fact that the supervisors raised the issue of plagiarism shows that other people, too, could reasonably think of that act in connection with the students' source use. As already noted, two of the supervisors addressed that point directly. Dr Morse said that others would call the source use of his writers 'minor plagiarism', and although she herself called Graciela's problems with source use 'small scale', Jenny Cain believed that 'there is some interpretation involved. I think some people might be much stricter, others might be more lenient still'. She also thought that Maria's source use was misleading in effect (although not by design), since it gave the impression that Maria had read sources which Cain tended to believe she had not. Frost said that by the rules provided to writers by his department, what Ingrid had done constituted plagiarism.

The risk that someone who did not know the readers might call their work plagiarism is to some extent a theoretical one. Master's theses (and indeed even PhD theses) do not typically have a wide readership. Yet even if the risk were small, the consequences for the writers would have been serious, and arguably unfair if deceptive intent did not lie behind the source use. A small risk, therefore, is still one to take seriously. More importantly, though, because the supervisors had not detected the source use they were unhappy with (until our interviews), they were not in a position to discuss it with the students. In the ordinary course of events, therefore, the master's students would have finished their degrees (just as the PhD writers appear to have done) without learning that their source use could be called plagiarism. If they continued to use the same source use strategies—and there is every reason to think they would—the likelihood of later detection would be higher, and the potential consequences steeper.

Identifying Problematic Source Use

Why did the inappropriate source use escape detection by the supervisors? Most fundamentally, because of the occluded relationship between the sources and the texts the students produced. Of course, the barrier of occlusion could have been circumvented, as it was in the interviews. The supervisors could have compared their students' writing to their sources, but it is hardly surprising that they did not. Time constraints militate against such an approach; as Dr Frost noted, 'you've got half an hour for each project report, there's no way most people would have the time to go back and check to what extent this sort of straight copying has occurred'. In addition, if the supervisors associated patch writing with plagiarism (as it appears they did at some level), they would be less likely to suspect, and check for, the presence of inappropriate source use in the work of students they knew and trusted. Frost recognized, and was concerned about, the difficulties of detection:

> What has always concerned me about this, as I've said, I'm quite confident that it is very, very common, I have absolutely no doubts that it's very common. But I think the problem with it is that only a handful of staff would ever have the time or the patience to spot it. And therefore . . . the criticism and identification falls very heavily on a few people who are unlucky enough to have written the work for someone who has this degree of care, patience and time to be able to check. And it's always worried me, I'm sure that the other ninety-five percent are also probably more or less equally to blame, they just haven't been spotted . . . It's not to say that I think it's right that you should do it but I think the punishments are very hard, given that it's very difficult to detect the crime.

There are, of course, occasions when, even without consulting a student's sources, a teacher may be alerted to the presence of source-dependent language by the presence of obtrusive 'seams' holding the pieces in the patchwork together, or by an awareness of an unusual degree of linguistic sophistication. Erden's and Roula's supervisors both commented on portions of the writing samples which they thought may have come from sources, although neither had taken steps to check. On the other hand, three of the supervisors did not identify extracts from their own publications in their students' texts. The teacher's instinct is, therefore, not always reliable, and some inappropriate source use will inevitably escape identification.

Individual Responses

As has been seen, the supervisors' responses to the opaque source use were varied. To some extent this was because the students' work was equally varied. That Jenny Cain responded differently to Graciela's source use than to Maria's was at least in part because the two writers used sources in qualitatively different ways. However, the supervisors' reactions also evidence differences in what they expected and valued.

A case in point is the emphasis that two supervisors, Wolfe and Vane, placed on the fact that their students had not engaged critically with their sources (as two of the writers in Abasi et al., 2006, had not). Dr Vane was concerned about several issues to do with source use in Pierre's writing sample, including the fact that he had very few references, but he highlighted the lack of discussion:

> A typical problem or a common problem among students is that they will read a reference but not review it, and they will copy extracts from it or summaries but they will not criticize it in anyway. This is not untypical. So he's used bits of information, put it down, in this case very limited, he hasn't bothered to say what he thinks of it, or whether they're right, wrong, and what are the reasons, why it should be different, anything like that.

Roula's supervisor was concerned about a similar lack of a critical approach to her sources. As an example of that tendency, he pointed out that she refers in one part of her writing sample to metonymy and metaphor as two of four categories of figurative language, but elsewhere describes metonymy as a subcategory of metaphor.

> So that is an example of what I mean by going through the motions. She's obviously done the research, she'd done the reading, she's reporting on the reading, but she hasn't synthesized it into a whole, it's a collection of bits.

Roula had not provided a reference for her classification of figurative language, and I asked Wolfe whether she ought to have:

NW: This is part of secondary school upbringing in a way and so for her to state categorically that there are these categories is not particularly problematic. I'm not too bothered in a sense about whether she attributes or not, except that I think she, from what I know of her, I think she's simply taken it lock stock and barrel from somewhere.
DP: Have you any idea from where?
NW: Not off the top of my head. It's not tremendously important because it's not controversial, the problem is that she ends up contradicting herself, and therefore her authorial responsibility is shot to pieces. She shoots herself in the foot.
DP: Okay . . . she doesn't need to provide authority for what she says here but she-
NW: If she had it would simply be a sort of honest reflection of where she got it from, if she doesn't it is on the borderline between general knowledge and particular attribution. I wasn't too bothered about that, in the end I'm not particularly bothered whether she says metonymy is a kind of metaphor or not as long as whatever view she holds is expressed consistently.

Several features about Roula's source use attracted Wolfe's notice: she did not give references for her classification of figures of speech, but the ideas themselves did not necessarily need references; they were 'on the borderline between general knowledge and particular attribution'. On the other hand, in this particular case a reference might have been in order because Wolfe thought Roula had taken her material 'lock stock and barrel' from somewhere. A citation, then, would be an 'honest reflection of where she got it from'. Wolfe tended, though, to dismiss those issues, giving greater emphasis to the theme he keeps returning to, what Roula actually argues. Whether she decides to class metonomy as a subcategory of metaphor or as a different kind of figurative language is not important 'as long as whatever view she holds is expressed consistently'. But since she is not consistent, 'her authorial responsibility is shot to pieces. She shoots herself in the foot'.

Vane and Wolfe were almost certainly not alone in wanting their students to engage with their sources, but they were the only two supervisors who brought the issue up in our interviews. There are a number of possible reasons why the other supervisors did not do so, one of which is that they did not see the issue as *unimportant* in regard to their students' work, but that other issues seemed more important. In any event, the fact that these two supervisors placed a greater emphasis on a critical relationship to sources than the others in our interview may reflect the kind of feedback they gave their students.

A more direct comparison can be made between the responses of the two biology supervisors. Ingrid's source use strategies in (67) are roughly similar to those of Erden in (64) above. Like Erden, Ingrid condensed the source, omitting parts (indicated in (67b) by an ellipsis). Both writers named their source but did not indicate that they repeated language from it. Ingrid made some changes in the last sentence, changing the order of 'also', and changing 'QTL' (qualitative trait loci) to 'loci'. Erden also reworded the last sentence somewhat.

67a Voorrips *et al.* (1997) mapped <u>two genes for resistance to clubroot (*Plasmodiophora brassicae*). A genetic map covering 615 cM in 12 linkage groups was assembled based on 92 RFLP and AFLP markers segregating in a population of 107 doubled haploid lines (DH lines) of *Brassica oleracea*. Resistance was determined in two ways: by assigning symptom grades to each plant, and by measuring the fresh weights of the healthy and affected parts of the root system to each plant. Two loci for clubroot resistance</u> were <u>found using a multiple QTL mapping approach to analyse the fresh weight data. The additive affect of these loci was responsible for 68% of the difference between the parents and for 60% of the genetic variance among DH-line means. Indications for the presence of two additional, minor</u> loci <u>were also found.</u>

[Ingrid]

67b Mapping of <u>two genes for resistance to clubroot (*Plasmodiophora brassicae*)</u> in a population of doubled haploid lines of Brassica oleracea by means of RFLP and AFLP markers . . . <u>A genetic map covering 615 cM in 12 linkage groups was assembled based on 92 RFLP and AFLP markers</u>

> segregating in a population of 107 doubled haploid lines (DH lines) of *Brassica oleracea* . . . <u>Resistance</u> in the DH-line population <u>was determined in two ways: by assigning symptom grades to each plant, and by measuring the fresh weights of the healthy and affected parts of the root system of each plant</u>. <u>Using a multiple QTL mapping approach to analyse the fresh weight data</u>, we <u>found two loci for clubroot resistance</u>: these were designated pb-3 and pb-4. <u>The additive effects of these loci were responsible for 68% of the difference between the parents and for 60% of the genetic variance among DH-line means</u>. Also, <u>indications for the presence of two additional, minor</u> QTLs <u>were found</u>.
>
> [Voorrips et al., 1997, p. 75]

As shown above, Dr Brown took issue with Erden's source use, but condemned it in hypothetical terms, saying that it would be important if it occurred repeatedly, and in the discussion section. Ingrid's supervisor was much more disapproving: 'they're told they should not have straight quotations of this sort'. The message from Ingrid's supervisor was, therefore, that this source use strategy was wrong, while the much more restrained message from Erden's was that it could be wrong in some contexts. Yet the two writers had done nearly exactly the same thing, in nearly exactly the same circumstances.

These differences in the supervisors' evaluation of similar source use are not highlighted in order to suggest that one was right and the other wrong, but to make two closely related points. First, such differences increase the insecurity for novice academic writers. If Erden continues to write in the way that Dr Brown found acceptable (if barely so), and finds himself in a situation in which Dr Frost evaluates his writing (if, for example, Erden submits a paper to a research journal and Dr Frost is asked to referee it), the result could be an accusation of plagiarism which Erden's academic training would not have prepared him to expect.

The second point is that the supervisors' different conclusions came out of fundamentally different perspectives on the rules that applied. Frost based his criticisms of Ingrid's work on the rules in effect in his department, rules which resemble those in effect in many university contexts, and which would be uncontroversial in most.

He read from those rules in our interview and concluded that under them, Ingrid's work should be called plagiarism. Brown, however, seemed to be drawing on unwritten rules and an informal sense of common practices when he said about Erden's source-dependent writing that 'coming up where it is, I think you would overlook it. If it was to come up in the discussion it would be an entirely different matter'.

The rules that Frost referred to say 'if you wish to transcribe word for word another person's writing, this should be in the form of a quotation with an appropriate introduction and reference, e.g. . . .' and an example in which quotation marks are used follows. Frost believed that this gave Ingrid a viable alternative; she could have signalled her quotation: 'she'd be at liberty to do that if she had put it in quotes'. Brown, however, said that people in their field do not quote:

> No, quotation is very, very rarely used at this level. You find that undergraduates use quotations a bit more cause it's perhaps a slightly easy way out, but at this level you would very rarely see quotation unless it was a very important point that some eminent scientist had come up with in the past. Otherwise you wouldn't see it.

The two supervisors had reached different conclusions about their students' source use through different routes, and each seemed confident that his conclusion rested on a solid foundation. This illustrates the need for a conversation in the academy and its disciplines about what academic writers are really expected to do—and why.

Several of the supervisors expressed unease that they had not discovered their students' dependence on the language of their sources. Dr Morse's explanation for his discomfort may reflect what other supervisors felt as well: 'it's unnerving because of the professionalism of the whole thing, because you feel, God, I should have read that article, been aware that it's been lifted from that article'. That response provoked in me a symmetrical sense of discomfort caused by my failure to anticipate that reaction. In planning this research I had given considerable thought—I believed sufficient thought—to the ethical consequences of conducting research on a sensitive topic like plagiarism. I considered possible consequences for the students, took steps to protect their privacy, and planned and conducted the interviews conservatively, avoiding lines of questions that might be interpreted as criticism or accusation, or that might otherwise make participants feel uncomfortable. Amid those considerations it did not occur to me that the supervisors might feel responsible for the students' source use, and therefore experience the same discomfort I was at pains to avoid for the students.

I understand, though, why I did not anticipate this reaction: I did not think, and do not think now, that it is justified. The supervisors who took part in this study were not negligent; nor were their supervision practices substandard in any way that the study revealed. The problem (to the extent that textual plagiarism is a problem) lay not in the supervisors, nor in the writers, but at the intersection of several factors: that it is difficult to identify how writers use their sources, that there is a lack of consensus in the academic community about what sorts of intertextuality are acceptable in practice and that the lack of consensus is masked by a superficial agreement at a more general level. This intersection exists inside the academic community, and so it is within that context that the problems, solutions and implications must be considered. That is the topic of the next chapter.

7

Plagiarism, patchwriting and source use in context

The focus of this book so far has been to analyse textual plagiarism as a linguistic phenomenon: as a phenomenon which results in a particular constellation of textual features, which is explained by conscious and unconscious choices made by writers and which contributes to the way the text will be received by its readers. Like all discoursal phenomena, textual plagiarism is affected by, and exerts effects on, the world around it. The purpose of this chapter is to connect the ideas raised so far with the academic context in which they are situated.

Three problems related to textual plagiarism have been identified. First, it has been seen to be a widespread but underdiagnosed phenomenon; second, patchwriting is often conflated with prototypical plagiarism; and third, there is little agreement in practice within the academic community about what is and is not plagiarism. These three problems taken together mean that the handling of textual plagiarism (the response to it when it is identified as well as efforts to address it proactively) is often less than optimal. Problems with source use are not consistently identified. When they are, a distinction is not always drawn between patchwriting and prototypical plagiarism, so the remediations may be inappropriate. This is unfair for students who are punished for plagiarism when other instances of plagiarism escape detection. It is unfair for students whose work is best described as patchwriting, but who are punished as deceptive plagiarists. But it is arguably least fair for students whose textual plagiarism is not identified, and who leave the university unaware that their ways of using sources are potentially problematic. They may go on to use the same strategies in contexts where the penalties can be steeper still.

This chapter presents ways of addressing textual plagiarism, both by teaching students effectively about writing from sources, and by responding to textual plagiarism in a consistent and equitable way, in the classroom and institutionally. The third section touches on a specific kind of response to plagiarism, electronic detection tools. The following two sections discuss issues of relevance for the global academic community and the changing university. Finally, areas in need of further investigation are identified.

Teaching about Plagiarism

A central argument in this book has been that textual plagiarism and source use should be the focus of explicit instruction. A useful tool for planning effective instruction is constructive alignment (Biggs, 1996). The alignment referred to is among educational objectives, instructional methods and assessment; simply put, constructive alignment means planning instruction and learning activities so that they relate to course objectives, and planning assessment so that it relates to what was taught.

A first essential step in applying the principles of constructive alignment to teaching about source use and textual plagiarism is to make those topics explicitly stated learning objectives. This is reasonable only if a formal distinction is made between prototypical plagiarism and patchwriting. Prototypical plagiarism is a form of cheating, an exercise in circumventing assessment, not something about which a learning objective can easily be formulated (*Upon completion of this course, students will be able to . . .?*). Patchwriting, however, is the result of a lack of fluency in the skill of writing on academic topics and drawing on other texts to do so, and a skill that is, and can be expressed as, a sensible course objective: *Upon completion of this course the student should be able to use and cite material from reference sources transparently.*

In teaching about source use, a useful framework for the facts students must learn is the idea of transparency (Chapter 4). Students' questions about sources often expect a simple yes-or-no answer (*Do I have to give a reference when I use this term? Can I use an example which came from a book, or should I make up my own?*). However, the answers to questions like that are often not simple. Whether a term requires a reference depends on its status—whether it is associated with a particular individual or has passed into the common domain—and deciding that requires an understanding of what the anticipated readers are likely to know about the term and its history of usage. More useful for students, therefore, than an answer to 'can I' and 'must I' questions, is a tool for finding the answers, to both current and future questions.

Transparency provides this tool by placing source use in context and causing the writer to reflect on his or her processes, and the reader's likely reactions. The counter-question to *Do I have to provide a reference?* is *If you don't, will it be clear to your reader how you've used your sources?* One way of raising awareness of transparency is to ask students to read each other's texts and comment on the ways they understand sources have been used. If the reader draws the conclusions that the writer intended, then transparency has been achieved. Teachers can include their assumptions about source use in their comments on student writing: *I understand that this idea comes from Cheddar, 2000, but that you've expressed it in a new way. Is that right?* This approach benefits more than source use skills; considering transparency forces writers to consider the reader's perspective, always a useful exercise for a writer.

Within the framework of transparency, specific points about the language of citation can be taught; a number of good writing books provide a review of citation forms, reporting verbs, etc. (e.g. Swales and Feak, 2004). For the mechanics of citation, a style manual commonly used in the discipline in question is a useful resource (e.g. the *Publications Manual of the American Psychological Association,* or the *Modern Language Association Handbook*).

However, while a body of declarative knowledge related to source use exists and should be taught, it is important to remember that writing from sources is primarily a skill. Constructive alignment requires learning activities to be relevant to objectives. If learning transparent source use is an objective, students need learning activities which make them practice and develop the skills involved in working with source texts. Writing tasks should be graded so that they are appropriate to learners' abilities, and become successively more difficult.

For example, writing a summary is a simpler task than synthesizing the views of half a dozen writers on a single topic.

In the legitimate peripheral participation model (Chapter 3), the learner has the opportunity to observe a more skilled practitioner performing the task. The difficulty of modelling the process of writing from sources has already been noted; however, teachers can ensure that their own teaching practices observe the same principles they want learners to apply to source use (Alexander, 1988) and by striving for originality in setting assignments. Some tasks are unlikely to elicit an original response: 'The assignment to write 1000 or 5000 words "on" Robert Frost or T. S. Eliot is itself a "plagiarized" assignment (i.e. one totally devoid of originality), and it invites the same in return' (Martin, 1971, p. 625). Or, in other words, 'If an assignment can be downloaded from the internet, perhaps it should be' (Sokolik, 2000).

Teachers can also model aspects of the process. 'Writing from sources' is shorthand for a number of micro-skills which make up the process, and which can be practiced. These include enclosing verbatim language in quotation marks and placing citations in the appropriate place and format (Whitaker, 1993; Wilhoit, 1994); note-taking, summarizing and paraphrasing (Kirkland and Saunders, 1991; Nienhuis, 1989; Sherman, 1992; Stahl and King, 1991; Zarpetea-loannou, 1998) and recognizing the arguments in other texts (Kantz, 1990; Sherman, 1992).

Assessment should also be in alignment with learning objectives and activities; in terms of source use, it means that students' attempts to write from sources must be assessed, and on formative assessment activities in particular students should receive feedback which comments directly on their source use. This requires, of course, that teachers actually be able to see how their students have used sources, so assessment activities must be planned to circumvent the problem of occlusion. One way of achieving this is to set assignments which ask students to draw on a narrow range of sources, known to the teacher (Whitaker, 1993). Another is to ask students to provide their sources, or at least some of them, and either hand them in together with a writing assignment or bring them to a writing conference (Wilhoit, 1994). If this is done after a preliminary draft of a writing assignment and before the final draft is due, students have every incentive to cooperate by supplying their sources and flagging potential problems for discussion.

    A final point following from the idea of constructive alignment is the weight that should be given to source use. Plagiarism has a tendency to assume larger-than-life proportions and take on a degree of importance that outweighs other considerations. As Buranen (1999) observes, 'no one comes quite so unglued about late papers or mistakes in subject/verb agreement. In fact, it is not hard to imagine that a student could quite easily receive less punishment for failing to turn in a paper at all than for turning in one that is "plagiarized"' (p. 72). If using sources effectively and appropriately is a curricular objective, then it is presumably one of many, and textual plagiarism should not override all other concerns. Similarly, it is important not only to comment on source use problems, but on successes as well. In addition, source use should be connected to other successful and less successful features of the text. It was seen in Chapter 4 that it is difficult to rely too much on the language of sources without relinquishing authorial control of a text. By pointing out features like the absence of a clear argument and relating them to source-dependent language, teachers can provide an incentive for transparent, effective source use that goes beyond simply avoiding plagiarism.

    To teach about source use effectively, students and teachers must work together on writing from sources, and collaborate to identify and fix problems. A precondition is that three assumptions must be shared by everyone in the classroom. The first two are that some textual plagiarism is not a mark of moral failure, and that, however important it is to detect and punish prototypical plagiarism (and it is indeed important), that goal should not be allowed to override the business of teaching and learning. A legitimate concern about plagiarism can be carried to a harmful extreme. Murphy (1990) writes about being thoroughly convinced that a student's work was plagiarized, and pursuing the matter to a point at which the student repudiated what later proved to be her own text. When a teacher raises a specific point about source use, if the writer perceives it as an accusation of wrongdoing, the effect on the learning process is detrimental (Petrić, 2004). To avoid collateral damage to the atmosphere of trust in the classroom—an atmosphere which is necessary if students are to feel free to draw attention to their source use by asking questions and inviting feedback—teachers must learn to avoid the emotional response of betrayal that discovering textual plagiarism can provoke (e.g. Bowden, 1996; Kolich, 1983).

A third fundamental assumption is that writing discipline-appropriate texts is a legitimate objective of any university classroom. This assumption is all too rare; instead, writing courses compete for room in the curriculum with 'content' courses and objectives within the latter are more likely to relate to 'content' than to ways of expressing it. The oversimplified (but often adopted) distinction between content and writing skills is impractical, though. Academic writing is discipline-specific (although of course similarities across disciplines exist, and writing skills are transferable). An approach to teaching writing, and source use, that relies exclusively on a Freshman Composition course, or sending students off to the writing centre (e.g. Ballard and Clanchy, 1991) will give students only limited help in learning how writing is done in their discipline. (This is not, of course, to suggest that writing centres or classes are not valuable tools, but merely that there are limitations on what they can accomplish.)

The problem is not only, or even primarily, that writing teachers are unfamiliar with conventions in other disciplines. Not every writing teacher knows that direct quotation is rare among natural scientists, but any writing teacher could learn this fact. More fundamentally, the ways that writing is done in the disciplines has a direct relationship to the ways that knowledge in those disciplines is constructed. Erden's and Ingrid's supervisors, both established researchers in the same area, disagreed about the acceptability of repeating language from a source. Their disagreement could only be meaningfully resolved through a discussion in their discipline; students need to learn the skills of writing from someone who is engaged in that conversation.

Institutional Responses

Academic institutions—departments, universities and intermediate structures—can do a great deal to facilitate pedagogical approaches to plagiarism. One important role they can perform is to ensure the availability of resources—time, above all—to allow teachers to do the things mentioned in the preceding section. Another is to ensure that the response to plagiarism is consistent and fair across the university. Many educational administrators are likely to see that as a role they already perform. Universities or their component units commonly have plagiarism policies and prescribe procedures for handling cases of suspected plagiarism. However, those policies ordinarily exist within the framework of the university's disciplinary rules, and are thus better suited to dealing with prototypical plagiarism than patchwriting. Institutional support is particularly needed in four areas: (1) identifying textual plagiarism; (2) distinguishing patchwriting from prototypical plagiarism; (3) providing options for responding pedagogically to plagiarism and (4) having sensible admission policies.

Identifying Textual Plagiarism

The responsibility for identifying textual plagiarism lies primarily with teaching staff. However, as has been seen, identification can be difficult, and institutions can play a role by providing teachers with the necessary support to identify source use problems. The higher the proportion of problems that are identified, the more effective teachers can be in improving students' skills. Finding textual plagiarism (and other problems) is therefore closely related to quality in education. One increasingly common approach to identifying plagiarism is the use of electronic detection systems, and these are discussed in the following section. Such systems have a number of drawbacks as well as advantages. Institutions can play an important role in seeing that there is a university-wide discussion about their use, and ensuring that, if implemented, they are used in a way that is pedagogically appropriate and fair.

Distinguishing between Patchwriting and Deceptive Plagiarism

The distinction between patchwriting and prototypical plagiarism is one of intent: one writer sets out to deceive; the other does not. At the institutional level, support for teaching staff in making this important determination can be achieved in several ways. It is important to ensure that teachers across the university are aware of the existence of separate forms of textual plagiarism. This is yet another aspect in which the response to student plagiarism is varied. Many teachers have experience of patchwriting as a strategy and are prepared to work with students on their source-dependent writing, but not all share that awareness. In addition, some teachers are willing to see source use problems as the result of a lack of declarative knowledge about what plagiarism is, and are therefore willing to explain to students that their textual plagiarism is not acceptable, but see a 'repeat offence' as a sign of intentional deception.

Teachers who accept that non-deceptive plagiarism exists must decide—in order to respond to it—which category an individual case falls into. Institutions can ensure fairness by reminding teachers that in the case of plagiarism, as in the case of any other sort of suspected wrongdoing, the presumption of innocence should apply. 'They must have known' is a common refrain when plagiarism is discovered, yet the evidence of this study along with many others cited in Chapter 1 is that 'they' often do not. There is, therefore, no reason to treat deceptive plagiarism as the default assumption. Spreading this message, and raising awareness of the issue, is a valuable step in ensuring that students across the university are treated consistently and equitably.

Responding to Textual Plagiarism

Institutional policies often address plagiarism in tones that state explicitly or suggest that they are concerned with the intentional form of the act (Pecorari, 2001). Further, it is not unusual for policies to stipulate procedures for responding to plagiarism which take the matter out of the teacher's hands. For teachers to have the freedom to deal pedagogically with patchwriting, as well as the resources to do so, university policies must recognize non-deceptive plagiarism and specify ways of addressing plagiarism that are responsive to the root causes (Howard, 1995, provides a model of what such a policy might look like; Yancey and Spooner, 1998, have shown the discouraging effects of some plagiarism policies).

Student Admissions

Policy makers can reduce the amount of textual plagiarism through the admission process. Patchwriting is a pervasive feature of the work of novice writers and is therefore to be expected in student writing. However, to the extent that it comes about when students' skills are not equal to the task at hand (or when students do not perceive that they are), the greater the gap between students' abilities and the expectations placed upon them, the more likely it is to occur and the more difficult it will be for students to learn to write in more autonomous ways.

Changes to higher education in recent decades have resulted in a more diverse student body. This means on one hand that fewer assumptions can be made about students and their backgrounds when they enter university, and on the other that some students may need extra support in learning to write from sources (among other things). Ensuring that students have reasonable chances of success on the courses they are admitted to, and the necessary support to remedy any deficits, is one valuable contribution educational administrators can make to an effective response to plagiarism.

Electronic Plagiarism Detection

A growing number of electronic plagiarism detection tools are in use at universities around the world. Given the difficulty of detecting plagiarism, and the importance of identifying it in order to be able to respond pedagogically, these tools are an attractive option for many teachers and universities. However, their use is associated with a number of problems, including the following (see Hayes and Introna,

2005, and Introna et al., 2007, for more about electronic detection systems in practice).

- Electronic detection packages can only identify electronic sources; textual plagiarism based on print sources will not be found.
- Nor will they identify all electronic sources. Information from password-protected databases (such as the ones students might access through their university libraries) will not be found; nor will the text of essays sold by 'paper mills', which some deceptive plagiarists purchase and submit as their own work.
- Because of the impossibility of comparing the full text of all student essays submitted to an electronic detection service to the full text of all the other documents stored in the service's databases and on the internet, detection software typically makes a 'digital fingerprint' for each document to be compared. Because the comparison is not made with the whole document, it is possible for some copying from sources to escape detection[1].

Electronic detection systems do not, therefore, find all instances of textual plagiarism. Is it nonetheless worth using them for the sake of those cases they do identify? One consideration is the cost–benefit relationship: what could be accomplished if the same resources were invested in expanding staffing at the writing centre, or used to provide a unit in effective and transparent source use in existing writing classes? In addition to this financial consideration, two other questions should be taken into account.

The first is how detection tools will be implemented in the classroom. As all responsible providers advise, detection systems are not intended as a substitute for good judgement and individual evaluation of student writing. The quantitative measures of similarity they provide are intended to alert teachers to a potential problem, not issue a verdict about whether plagiarism is present in a text. However, there is anecdotal evidence that the message does not always reach the front lines, and that some teachers use the reports of comparisons mechanically, implementing formulae such as lowering an essay by a letter grade if the similarity to source reaches a certain threshold, or giving a failing grade if it reaches a certain higher threshold. This potential for misuse is not a criticism of detection systems in itself, but it does suggest that plans for ensuring good practice should go hand in hand with a decision to adopt an electronic tool.

Of at least equal importance is the message the use of such tools sends to students. There is a real risk that the backwash effect can cause students to devote their attention and energy to lowering their 'plagiarism score' by substituting synonyms and making other superficial changes rather than concentrating on using sources effectively and following the principle of transparency. The risk also exists that students can see the use of plagiarism detection software as evidence that their teachers and institutions mistrust them, something which is never helpful to the learning process but which in the specific case of teaching writing from sources would make open discussions about how sources have been used difficult if not impossible.

There is also a need to question what message electronic detection systems send students about intellectual property and the rights of authors. The largest services not only compare student work to the internet, they have a database of student writing for comparison. As each writing assignment is compared, it is also added to the database. This is an important element in the commercial success of such companies, since the larger their database, the more useful the tool. There is, however, an irony in a response to plagiarism (an act which is commonly viewed as an infringement of the author's rights) which causes students to relinquish control over their own texts.

This is the view taken by a group of students at a US secondary school, who at the time of writing were suing a prominent provider of plagiarism detection services. Their attorney was quoted in the press as saying, 'The problem with [the service] is the archiving of the documents. They are violating a right these students have to be in control of their own property' (Glod, 2007). Before taking this step, the students organized a petition in their school against the service, and got over 1000 signatures (Glod, 2006). The merits of the lawsuit aside, the reaction of these students is highly significant: any step that causes students to feel this degree of discomfort is one that educators should think very carefully about before taking.

The Global Academic Community

In late 2007 a public episode of plagiarism was reported in *Nature*. A scientist commenting on the case called the source use of the writers involved 'dishonest and sloppy' ('Turkish physicists face accusations of plagiarism', 2007, p. 8). A later issue featured a letter to the editor from one of the scientists involved, defending his source use practices. He wrote:

> For those of us whose mother tongue is not English, using beautiful sentences from other studies on the same subject in our introductions is not unusual. I imagine that if all articles from specialist fields of research were checked, similarities with other texts and papers would easily be found. . . . Borrowing sentences in the part of a paper that simply helps to better introduce the problem should not be seen as plagiarism. Even if our introductions are not entirely original, our results are—and these are the most important part of any scientific paper.
>
> (Yilmaz, 2007, p. 658)

The sincerity of explanations brought forward by an accused party to mitigate guilt is always subject to scepticism. However, this scientist's explanation coincides neatly with the findings of a study carried out by Flowerdew and Li (2007). They investigated the source use practices of PhD students who were non-native speakers of English, and found that among their frequent strategies was the repetition of language from sources without attribution—textual plagiarism. However, this did not come about by accident, oversight or wilful intention to deceive; the writers defended their strategies as an appropriate way to produce linguistically competent texts.

This illustrates the range of views in the academic community as to what constituted plagiarism and appropriate source use (also noted by Errey, 2002, and Roig, 2001). The lack of practical consensus handicaps efforts to teach students what constitutes good and legitimate use of sources, since those who are doing the teaching are not always in agreement, nor aware of the differences. A conversation in the academic community is therefore badly needed. Because plagiarism is a polarizing issue, the conversation must not be framed as supporters of academic standards versus advocates of leniency, and because plagiarism is so closely linked to the context in which it occurs, the conversation cannot be based on the assumption that there is a single right solution to the problem.

More than ever before, the academic community is an international one, and the conversation about source use and plagiarism should be as well. It is an interesting feature of this international community that its lingua franca, English, is also the local language of several countries which have been prominent in the internationalization of academic life. International students are central to the economies of universities in countries like Britain, the United States and Australia, in part because the fact of a degree having been earned in English gives it added value. English is the language of publication for journals with an international reputation, and non-native speakers are at a disadvantage in comparison to native speakers in having their research published (Flowerdew, 2000). The status of English in the global academic community is, in a word, special.

To the extent that there may be local variations in source use practices, it is imperative that the conversation about standards for source use be one in which a range of voices are heard, and that any answers that emerge from it should reflect consensus, rather than the local standards of the English-speaking world being imposed on the rest of the academic community.

The University of the Future

Higher education is changing rapidly for reasons including the expanding proportion of the population participating in higher education, growth in distance instruction supported by information technology and the increasing number of people travelling abroad to study. Changes to educational structures and the participants in them will necessarily affect how plagiarism and related issues are viewed and dealt with. In this section two issues which are especially relevant to the changing face of the university will be addressed: the role of the internet, and the commodification of higher education.

Plagiarism and the Internet

It is a commonplace that the increasing availability of electronic technology, in particular the internet, has caused an increase in plagiarism. It is suggested that electronic media make more information more easily accessible to students, and it need not even be retyped; the relevant pieces can be copied and pasted into another document. 'Paper mills' selling writing assignments on the internet make it easier still to obtain a completed writing assignment. The ability to make multiple copies of a document, perhaps with minor changes to its format, without the additional effort of retyping, facilitates collusion between students.

The connection between the internet and a supposed increase in plagiarism has been asserted so often in the press (e.g. DeGroot, 2000; Midgely, 2000; Porter, 2000) and even in academic journals (e.g. Austin and Brown, 1999) that it seems to have gained truth value simply through repetition. There is, however, ample reason to be sceptical about claims that the electronic media are responsible for a rise in plagiarism. Plagiarism, collusion and even paper mills predate the internet. Simmons traces a concern with student plagiarism back to the beginnings of academic writing instruction in the United States, in the nineteenth century (1999).

The supposed increase in plagiarism is asserted, rather than demonstrated. Most laments about internet plagiarism rely on anecdotal evidence of an increase, but a rise in the number of cases discussed around the photocopier or even the number of cases brought to disciplinary proceedings does not necessarily indicate an increase in plagiarism. As an alternative scenario, if there is a perception that plagiarism is on the rise, then teachers may be more proactive in trying to identify it, and that could lead to an increase in reported cases without any increase in the actual incidence. This is not to argue that there has *not* been an increase in plagiarism, but rather that there is insufficient evidence to decide the question either way.

It is clear, however, that the internet has changed the intertextual landscape irrevocably, and that the contours of the new landscape are not yet clarified. It has been noted that the development of electronic media has outpaced the relevant legislation, making a review of the relevant laws necessary (Larochelle, 1999, p. 121). The familiar boundaries between public domain and copyrighted material are less clear on the internet (Bloch, 2001). It has been argued that this is due in part to the newness of the electronic discourse community. Zebroski (1999) argues that collaboration is normative in new movements, while a sense of authorship develops when the movement becomes established, and suggests that among his undergraduates plagiarism is not due merely to the availability of electronic information, but also to the fact that the students, 'all intensively into computers . . . had been initiated not only into computer writing practices, but into this utopian ideology and its user community', and were therefore participating in a movement still in its collaborative phase (p. 39). Belcher shows that evaluating the reliability of information and its source is a more difficult task with material found on the internet. Hypertext makes authorship harder to distinguish, leading Belcher to wonder whether 'the internet and hypertext are actually undermining the print literacy notions of authorship that many writers and writing teachers subscribe to: our sense of authors as creators and authorizers of their own rhetorically motivated text, through which they are able, at least potentially, to exercise some influence over readers' (2001, p. 140). In summary, the rules of the game have changed, but have not yet stabilized. In this context it would be surprising if novice writers, who are in the process of learning the rules, did not find it a challenging task, and did not sometimes make inferences that are not widely shared by established members of their discourse communities.

These concerns are illustrated in the work of one of my students in an advanced English proficiency course who undertook a writing assignment on the topic—selected by him—of the Dogma school of filmmakers. While reading his text I formed the impression that parts of it—specifically the part that provided a 'boilerplate' description of who and what the Dogma school is—had come from other sources. I googled a phrase I thought might have been patchwritten, and found the phrase, somewhat to my surprise, not in one source but many. Some of the hits that were generated appear in (68)[2] (bold type has been added to indicate portions of the passage which are similar to, but not necessarily identical to, others of the examples).

68a Naturally, Søren Kragh-Jacobsen obeyed this rule while making *"Mifune"*—just as he has faithfully adhered to the other Dogma Commandments (now dubbed the 'Vow of Chastity') which **include the mandatory use of handheld cameras, a ban on artificial lighting and props brought in from off set, and insistence on a plot that takes place here and now, without "superficial action"** (i.e. no guns or murder).

68b The 10 rules of the Dogme 95 charter, drawn up by Danish directors Lars von Trier and Thomas Vinterberg **include the mandatory use of handheld cameras, a ban on artificial lighting and sound, and insistence on a plot that takes place here and now without containing superficial action.**

68c Dogme 95 is a naïve and self-gratifying cinematic movement founded by Dutch filmmakers Thomas Vinterberg, Lars Von Trier, Søren Kragh-Jacobsen, and Kristian Levring. Between them they drafted a(n oft-betrayed) manifesto dedicated to "rescuing" motion pictures from artifice **by forbidding special lighting, props brought in from off-site, advocating handheld camerawork, and urging an avoidance of recognizable genre definitions.** Too often that obsession with bypassing convention plays a little like a convention; over the course of eleven films it has defined a disquieting genre all its own.

68d Funny, romantic and a perfect antidote to all the hi-tech wizardry of "Lord of the Rings" or the stylised perfection of "Gosford Park". This is one of the set of films adhering to the **Dogma 95 rules which include use of handheld cameras, no artificial lighting or props brought in from off set and a plot that takes place here and now.** It sounds very "arty" but in fact it's delightfully watchable (though it is in Danish with English subtitles). If you're not a Woking library user you'll have to request it but what's an extra pound for an alternative to the average evening's TV offerings?

68e The Dogme film movement was established by a group of Dutch filmmakers in 1995, in part, as a response to the "failure" of the French New Wave movement of the '60s. The group's vows **(including the use of only hand-held cameras, no pre-recorded sound and no artificial lighting)**

68f The first American effort to be granted "Dogme95" status by a brotherhood of Dutch filmmakers (Thomas Vinterberg, Lars Von Trier, Søren Kragh-Jacobsen, and Kristian Levring) dedicated to rescuing motion pictures from the realms of artifice, Korine's *julien donkey-boy* is a grotesquely beautiful piece about family relationships. Although his movie adheres to Dogme95's demands of **no special lighting, no props not found at the site of filming, handheld camerawork, and an avoidance of recognizable genre,** the obvious manipulation of images in post-production seems to betray the theoretical purity of the group's mission statement.

Often the repeated language came from sections of websites which gave background information about the tenets of the Dogma 95 movement. (68a) comes from a text about the Søren Kragh-Jacobsen film *Mifune,* a text which was found in virtually identical form on four other sites. The first three sites end the text with a credit to an article by Ebbe Iversen in the Danish newspaper the *Berlingske Tidende.* The fourth gives no attribution at all. (68e) comes from a review of two Dogma 95 films, a review which appears on two web pages. The Center Stage website credits the review to a Paul Freitag, but only extensive exploration of the other site yielded the information that that site was maintained by (presumably the same) Paul Freitag.

Students who find sites such as these must be excused for drawing conclusions about the reusability of language which differ from what their composition teachers or thesis advisors might believe. Fairly long phrases are reused without attribution at all. Entire pieces of writing are reproduced, often in circumstances which suggest that it may have been done with permission and appropriately, but with the acknowledgement absent or minimized.

One of the findings of this study was that novice writers look to the texts they read as models. Writers who use internet texts may receive confusing information and mixed signals, much of it at odds with what the academic community at large finds acceptable. A challenge for the future is to respond to the influences of electronic media on what responsibility the academic writer has for attribution, and on the implications for learning about writing from sources.

The Commodification of Higher Education

One of the many changes in higher education has been its conversion into a product to sell. Fee-paying students have become customers. One group, in particular, international students, has become an important consumer base for universities in the English-speaking world and, increasingly, elsewhere in Europe. A study of the supervision process at British universities in the 1990s found that

> For some supervisors, the 'problem' with overseas students was not located in the students themselves, but in the questionable morality of university recruitment practices. They believed that the high tuition fees overseas students paid resulted in feverish attempts to attract such students and consequent pressures upon academic staff to take on their supervision. . . .
> (Acker et al., 1994, p. 491)

In the intervening years, the pressure on universities to admit international students has not diminished; nor has the report of resulting problems, as this piece from an Australian newspaper attests:

> Funding cuts have forced universities to take in large numbers of feepaying overseas students. They number about 240,000, or a quarter of the student body. Australia's international student industry . . . is worth $9.8 billion . . . The anger level of

English-as-first-language students is rising as lecturers "dumb down" their teaching for international students, who are left bewildered by the resentment they feel comes from the first-language English speakers—after all, the international students were actively recruited by the universities, and they sat language tests which led them to believe they could make it.

(Susskind, 2006)

This raises two related questions (neither of which is within the scope of this book to resolve, but which deserve attention). The first is whether it may not be in the interests of universities to keep paying customers happy. The approach to textual plagiarism suggested in the first part of this chapter is to allocate source use a place in the curriculum and teach and assess it properly. That would involve time, and time is money. However, if the alternative is a situation in which large numbers of students are presented with objectives they cannot reasonably attain, then such expenses might be seen in the light of an investment, a way of producing satisfied consumers.

The second and closely related question is what students might come to demand as they increasingly see themselves as customers, and pay increasingly high fees. Eight of the writers whose work was examined as part of this study completed PhD degrees. Given that the portions of their work considered here came from completed theses, it is likely that they still did not know, at the end of their studies, that their source use could potentially attract charges of plagiarism. The PhD is often pursued in preparation for an academic career, so it is not unlikely that some of those writers have gone on, or will go on, to publish, and to do so using sources in the same way. If plagiarism were to be identified in their work, the practical consequences could be crushing. At that point, they might reasonably wonder why the universities that took their tuition fees did not teach them a fundamental aspect of academic writing, nor notice when they demonstrated that they had not mastered it.

This was precisely the point made by an undergraduate at a British university who was on the eve of receiving his bachelor's degree when a routine review of his coursework revealed that he had plagiarized repeatedly over the years of his studies. According to press accounts (Baty, 2004; 'Plagiarising', 2004), the student acknowledged having copied from internet sources, but argued he had not known it was wrong. What the university saw as an aggravating circumstance, the fact that the textual plagiarism had continued throughout the student's years at university, was adduced by the student as a mitigating circumstance: he had consistently used the same strategy and no objections to it had been voiced earlier. The student was quoted as saying:

> I can see there is evidence that I have gone against the rules, but they've taken all my money for three years and pulled me up the day before I finished. If they had pulled me up with my first essay at the beginning and warned me of the problems and consequences, it would be fair enough. But all my essays were handed back with good marks, and no one spotted it.
>
> (Baty, 2004)

As a result, the student decided to sue his university.

Questions for Further Investigation

This investigation of student writing has touched on a number of issues about which too little is known. This section reviews questions for which satisfactory answers are not yet available, and which are promising areas for future research.

What Is Plagiarism?

This central question still cannot be answered in any comprehensive way. The superficial uniformity of definitions of plagiarism hides the diversity of specific practices. Any answer to the question must be based on consensus among members of the discourse community involved. A series of disciplinary conversations must be part of this, but research investigating what individual academics identify as plagiarism would be a useful reference point. Hyland points out that 'because texts are written to be understood within certain cultural contexts, the analysis of key genres can provide insights into what is implicit in these academic cultures, their routine rhetorical operations revealing individual writer's perceptions of group values and beliefs' (2000, p. 11). Understanding what specific textual acts constitute plagiarism will almost certainly be based on, and contribute to, an understanding of what things are valued in that field.

The Baby and the Bathwater

The classroom and institutional interventions proposed above are practical, workable approaches to limiting patchwriting, addressing it both proactively and after the fact. As a teacher I am comfortable proposing them as a solution to a specific problem: the existence of a way of writing (patchwriting) which is widely perceived as inappropriate, and which is risky for the writers who produce it. At another level, though, I am uncomfortable proposing solutions for an act, plagiarism, which has not been sufficiently problematized[3]. Many aspects of plagiarism deserve closer, critical scrutiny. I will illustrate that need here by examining a single unanswered, and indeed seldom asked, question: does patchwriting, along with other forms of repetition, serve a pedagogical function? If so, there is a possibility that when we block repetition as an approach to writing, we are throwing the baby out with the bathwater.

Hull and Rose studied a remedial, English L1 writer, Tanya, who drew on the language of her sources in a way that advanced her development as a writer, and concluded

> A powerful pedagogic next move with Tanya, then, would be temporarily to suspend concern about error and pursue, full tilt, her impulse to don the written language of another. What she seems to need at this point in her reentry into the classroom is a freewheeling pedagogy of imitation, one that encourages her to try on the language of essays. . . .
>
> (1989, p. 151)

Repetition, memorization and copying may be effective learning strategies (Buranen, 1999, p. 72; Cook, 1994; Murray, 1992), but they are not exploited by an academic community that values originality and for whom repetition is anathema. Swearingen wonders if there is not an alternative:

> How can paraphrase and imitation of styles be used without apology or questions of authenticity to prepare students to develop a diversity of voices in their repertoire? How can the proper uses of paraphrase and quotation be introduced as conventions of academic and nonacademic discourse in interesting and challenging ways, ways that encourage students to think about their own and others' boundaries of self, voice, authenticity, and indebtedness? Finally, how can the examples of our own Western, Eurocentric rhetorical traditions be placed alongside comparable intellectual and pedagogical traditions in our students' cultures so that the commonality of borrowings and voices, individualisms and collectivities, can be understood not as unbridgeable differences but as shared routes to speaking together, knowing, writing, and reading? If these are not the objectives of classroom discourses today, they should be.
>
> (1999, pp. 29–30)

Buranen supports this idea; the writers she worked with in a US community college used textual plagiarism, she argues, because they were writing within a context which placed too much emphasis on formal accuracy and denied them 'the opportunity to grapple with the real messiness of the writing process' (p. 74) and the learning that goes along with it. If Howard is right in saying that patchwriting is a stage through which all writers pass in the process of acquiring academic literacy (1999), then trying to cause a detour around it may ultimately not be productive.

This possibility was brought home to me quite vividly by my daughter. One afternoon when Chiara was 10, I sat in a local pizzeria with her and her friend Eleanor. The two girls attended different schools and over lunch they compared experiences. Their geography lessons, they found, took the same format. Each week they studied a county by reading a chapter in the textbook and then writing a short report. The format of the report was specified: there were to be sections about the official county plant and animal, and a larger section about other points of interest such as important industries or large cities.

The girls agreed that their teachers asked them *not* to copy from the geography book, but that nonetheless most people did, themselves included. They then concluded that writing their geography reports was boring. My suggestion—that it might be more interesting if they planned and produced their own texts, instead of copying—was not well received.

A short time later, though, Chiara had a learning conference and her teacher pointed out that although she knew it was common practice, the geography reports were not meant to be copied from the textbook. Thus feeling authorized to intervene, when the report was next on the homework agenda, I suggested a procedure: she read the book, and then closed it and noted down the relevant facts she remembered. Then she put her notepaper away and opened the book again for a second reading, followed by another round of adding to her notes. Eventually the notes formed the basis for her report.

The experiment was partially successful. Chiara enjoyed the writing process more, and devoted some thought to how to organize the information she wanted to include (the principle decision required by the copying strategy was what to leave out). However, the finished product differed significantly from others in the notebook in one respect: the language was poorer. Not only were there some orthographic and grammatical errors, her vocabulary was less varied and there were fewer high-register words and complex grammatical structures.

Was this a problem? If the report had been an assessment tool, then a finished product that reflected what Chiara could write on her own would have been more valuable than the copied version. But in the context of a learning activity, repeating language may have been a way of practicing using new words and structures, and without that practice, a chance to learn them may have been bypassed (Flowerdew and Li, 2007; Villalva, 2006). That was the point Roula's supervisor was making when he said: 'it's what I recommend students do. "Steal" the language. Don't steal the contents but steal the language. "Distinguishes between x and y"'.

Chunks of language like 'distinguishes between x and y' are a pervasive feature of the written and spoken production of native speakers and an element in making language use sound fluent (e.g. Wray, 2002). Estimates for the proportion of chunks of formulaic language vary, but may be as high as 58 per cent in spoken language and over 50 per cent in writing (Erman and Warren, 2000). In that light this example from SS2's text is interesting:

69a From the definitions presented above, the focal points for research are the collection of information, and the expansion of knowledge, and also the evaluation of them.
[SS2]

69b The research hypothesis, therefore, is the focal point of the quest for knowledge.[8]
[Wise et al., 1967, p. 10; the note gives a citation to Van Dalen]

SS2 had quoted from Wise immediately before the extract in (68a), and the part he quoted comes shortly before the text in (69b). A difference between Wise and SS2, though, is that Wise has *focal point* in the singular while the student made it plural. The plural form seemed, intuitively, the less likely choice, and a query to the British National Corpus confirmed that that is so: it gives 318 instances of 'focal point' and only 42 of 'focal points'. Not only are there fewer plural occurrences, they are often used differently. SS2 has a single entity, if an abstract one (research) possessing the focal points. Often, though, when the phrase is plural, as in (70), a number of entities (such as communities) each have a focal point.

70 Development of GP surgeries and health centres into "focal points", alongside improvements in nursing and residential care and community hospitals . . .

It is interesting to speculate whether SS2 came across the expression *focal point* in Wise's text, recognized it as a useful one and incorporated it into his own text, although in a less typical way.

This speculation raises a number of questions. Did the student writers see their use of language from sources in similar terms, i.e. as recycling functional chunks of language? The sort of formulaic chunks described by Wray (2002), Erman and Warren (2000) and others are considerably shorter, but the students may nonetheless have perceived their borrowing in that light. Is there a means of distinguishing between appropriate chunks and inappropriate repetition? Does the distinction lie in the process? Must new chunks enter the new text through what Wray (2002) terms 'the mental lexicon' rather than directly from another text? How successful are novice writers in importing formulaic chunks into their writing, so that the form and the meaning are a good fit? Do formulaic chunks come predominantly from some portions of a source, or go predominantly into some sections of the new text? All these questions are interesting areas for future investigation, along with the larger one with which this section began: does discouraging patchwriting have a negative effect on the acquisition of formulaic language?

Conclusion

Plagiarism is traditionally constructed as a problematic act. This book has attempted to highlight some of the problematic aspects of plagiarism in academic contexts. First, textual plagiarism can sometimes occur as an intentional violation of accepted conventions, but often has other causes. Next, the two sorts of plagiarism—the kind that is dishonest and the kind that is not—are difficult to distinguish between. One reason for this difficulty is the lack of agreement in the academic world about the specific source use practices that are considered appropriate, objectionable or somewhere in between. In addition, the lack of agreement on the specifics is masked by a uniform rhetoric around plagiarism at the general level. Then, crucially, the penalties for committing this act are heavy indeed. Plagiarism, then, is not a problem with a text, but a problem that arises from a gap between the kinds of texts that some writers produce, and the expectations of (some of) their readers, a gap which is all the more worrying because it is so often unrecognized.

In practical terms, plagiarism is a serious problem for individuals like the Turkish scientist and the British undergraduate referred to above, and was a potential problem for the students who took part in this study; it is imperative that a solution be found. One of the purposes of this book has been to demonstrate the need for a solution that does not oversimplify the complex issues involved. More effective detection methods are not enough when there is little agreement about what needs to be detected. Teaching novice academic writers about source use, a positive thing in itself, will run up against the same problem: what are students to be taught to do and not do? A solution which privileges native English speakers in the international academic community cannot be equitable, and probably would not be workable. A solution to the complex problems associated with plagiarism can only come about as a result of conversation in the academic community(ies), aimed at identifying the kinds of source use that best serve the needs of academic discourse, and the kinds of textual plagiarism which are (and are not) disruptive of the community's activities. Reaching consensus on issues like those is no easy objective, but the very attempt to reach it will be beneficial.

Notes

1. I am grateful to Lucas Introna for explaining the workings of plagiarism detection systems in a personal communication on 6 September 2007.
2. The examples in (68) were taken from the following sites:
    (a) http://www.spe.sony.com/classics/mifune/dogma95.html
    (b) http://www.kamera.co.uk/reviews_extra/mifune.php
    (c) http://www.filmfreakcentral.net/screenreviews/italianforbeginners.htm
    (d) http://ww2.surreycc.gov.uk/lib/hooked.nsf/96aa49a2886000 2 f80256a5d003a8fad/8e05fd0fd9b4f1bb80256b6b0066de05?OpenDocument
    (e) http://www.geocities.com/Hollywood/Movie/1754/mifuneidiots.html and http://www.centerstage.net/stumped/articles/dogme.shtml
    (f) http://filmfreakcentral.net/dvdreviews
    (g) http://hivebalur.net/bcp/reviews/juliendb.htm/juliendonkeyboy.htm
    (h) http://www.splicedonline.com/01reviews/kingisalive.html All were accessed on 27 April 2002.
3. At least, not by the wider academic community. This has happened in some areas, e.g. literary studies, through the works of authors such as Kathy Acker, Huber Aquin, Ricardo Piglia, Renaud Camus, Yambo Ouologuem (see, for example, Cosgrove, 1989; Force and Jullien, 1988; Friedman, 1989; McCracken, 1991; Randall, 1990, 1991; Sciolino, 1989, 1990).

Appendix: Research methods

The methods used in this investigation were presented briefly in Chapter 4. This appendix provides a more detailed description of the procedures for gathering and analysing the data.

Choice of Participants

The students whose texts were used in this study were all non-native speakers of English (NNSEs) and postgraduate students at British universities. The decision to work with NNSEs in this project was not made because there was any reason to think they are more likely to plagiarize than other students, but because source use is a language-sensitive matter, and homogeneity in the group of participants—that is, not mixing L1 and L2 speakers—was desirable. Both prototypical plagiarism and patchwriting are well attested in the work of native speakers (e.g. Howard, 1995, 1999, 2007).

The choice to use postgraduates as participants was made for several reasons. First, research writing tends to draw more intensively on sources than the types of assignments undergraduate are often given; there is more source use to study in theses. Secondly, theses can be considered a more 'authentic' text type than those that undergraduates write. Not only is the role of the thesis more crucial to the students' success than any other single text, students who continue to do research will have a similar need in their future publications to contextualize their work in the existing research literature. However, although they were postgraduates, it is fair to call these students novice academic writers. As they were all NNSEs, regardless of the writing experience they may have had in their first languages, they were less experienced in English. Of the nine writers who were interviewed, and about whom personal information is available, only Maria and Roula, who had earned BAs in Britain, and Erden, who had published research in his field, had experience of academic writing in English prior to beginning their courses. With the exception of Erden, who had published in Turkish as well as English, and Graciela, who had previously done a journalism degree in her country, the participants were not experienced writers even in their own languages. And even the most experienced of the group, Erden, reported that writing was the most challenging part of completing his thesis, 'because it's not my own language, first. And also I'm not good even in my own language in writing'. Since the PhD in Britain often involves no coursework, it is possible that some of that group actually had less academic writing experience than the master's students, many of whom wrote a certain number of long essays as part of their course.

The writers came from three universities which were selected for their strong reputations in both research and teaching. The writers in the two subcorpora—master's and PhD students—were identified in different ways. The supervisors were the most practical line of approach to the master's students, since they were easier to contact, and since their participation in the research would also be solicited. Initially I contacted 28 lecturers in a number of academic departments and explained the study in general terms as an investigation into the academic writing of international students. The message to supervisors gave an indication of what participation would entail, in terms of the time commitment and the nature of the involvement, and asked whether they would be willing to take part in the study, and if so, whether they had students who were international students and NNSEs engaged in writing a master's dissertation. The text of the message to lecturers appears in Figure A.1.

Six lecturers agreed to take part and had students who met these criteria. They furnished the names of 23 students whom I contacted, giving a general description of the study. The text of the message to students appears in Figure A.2.

Dear X,

I'm writing (at the suggestion of . . .) to ask if you would be willing to take part in a study I am carrying out as part of my work toward a PhD in the English Department at Birmingham University. The subject of my research is the writing process of international students working on their master's dissertations, and it involves looking at draft portions of dissertations and speaking to students and their supervisors about it.

Supervisors' participation consists of a one-hour interview and access to a draft chapter of the student's work with the supervisor's comments. The consent and participation of your student(s) would be sought too.

If you are supervising one or more international students and think you might be willing to take part, please let me know at [e-mail address]

or at the address below. If there are any questions you'd like answered before deciding, please feel free to ask me or my supervisor, [name and contact details were provided].

With thanks,

Diano Pocorari

[address and telephone number]

FIGURE A.1 *Message inviting supervisors to participate in the study.*

Nine students did not respond to either the first message or subsequent follow-up contacts, and one declined to take part in the study without giving a reason. Of the 13 students who initially agreed to be included, 4 did not complete the study: one did not supply a writing sample, two provided writing samples so close to the end of the research period that it was not possible to arrange interviews and one returned home for health reasons without completing her dissertation. The remaining nine students were in four subject areas, civil engineering, biology, education and linguistics, corresponding to Biglan's (1973a, 1973b) typology of hard versus soft and pure versus applied disciplines.

Dear X,

I've been given your name by your supervisor, XXX, who has agreed to take part in a study I am carrying out as part of my work toward a PhD in the English Department at the University of Birmingham. I'm writing to ask if you would be willing to participate in this project too.

If you agree, you would be asked to take part in two interviews of approximately one hour each, and to allow your supervisor to show me some of the writing you do for your dissertation.

If you decide to take part, I will provide you with more information about the research, including the scheduling of the interviews; in the meantime, if there are any questions I can answer, please let me know.

Best regards,

Diane Pecorari

[address, telephone number and e-mail address]

FIGURE A.2 *Message inviting students to participate in the study.*

After students and their supervisors agreed to involvement in the study, they were given an information sheet with greater detail about their involvement. The text of this information sheet appears in Figure A.3.

To protect the identity of the PhD students, no contact was to be made with them, and the process of identifying suitable texts somewhat simpler. Potentially suitable theses were identified from university library catalogues, taking three criteria into account: (1) that they maintained the spread of disciplines; (2) that they came from a relatively tight time period (between 1994 and 1999) given that conceptions of appropriate source use change across time (Bazerman, 1984; Salager-Meyer, 1999) and (3) that they were written by international students who were NNSEs.

What is involved if I participate in this study?

If you are a student, you will be asked to:

- take part in two interviews;
- agree to me talking to your supervisor about your writing;
- agree to your supervisor sending me a draft of part of your dissertation with his or her comments.

If you are a supervisor, you will be asked to:

- take part in one interview;
- send me a draft section of your student's dissertation, after you have commented on it.

What will the interviews involve?

Each interview will take about an hour. In the first interview, students will be asked about their experiences with academic writing. In the second interview, students and supervisors will be asked to talk separately about the student's writing.

I will ask permission at the beginning of the interview to make a tape recording of it. If this makes you uncomfortable, please say so.

Confidentiality and anonymity

Interviews with students and supervisors will take place separately. I will not repeat anything a student tells me to his or her supervisor, or vice versa, unless I specifically ask for, and receive, permission to do so.

Steps will be taken to protect the confidentiality of participants. In particular, the names of the universities, departments and individuals taking part will be changed. However, a small possibility remains that a student could be identified through background information or extracts from his or her writing. If you wish to say something that should NOT be reported, please tell me that you are speaking 'off the record' and I will respect your wishes.

Who will see my writing?

Because writing conventions can vary from field to field, I may show parts of writing samples to other experts in the same field–anonymously, of course.

Because I am a research student, I will make my data, including student writing samples, available to my supervisor. Extracts from writing samples, supervisors' comments, and statements from the interviews will be quoted in my dissertation and conference papers and publications stemming from it. I assume that by agreeing to take part in this project you give me permission to do these things. If you have questions about this, or are not sure you want me to use your writing in this way, please say so.

Possible issues arising from the research:

This research project will look closely at the academic writing of the students who take part. In the process, students and/or supervisors may become aware of areas of difficulty that they then feel need further work. In a pilot study, students and supervisors reported that this was positive, as it resulted in a stronger dissertation. It is, however, a possibility you need to be aware of.

I'll be very happy to explain anything that is not clear or is not covered in this information sheet–just ask!

Many thanks for your help.

Diane Pecorari

[address, telephone number and e-mail address]

FIGURE A.3 *Information sheet for students and supervisors.*

The final criterion was the most difficult to achieve without making contact with the writers or people who knew them. However, the students' names and thesis topics offered clues (for example, one wrote about Mandarin Chinese), and once eight candidates had been selected who seemed likely to be NNSEs, additional confirmation was found from a number of sources, including the acknowledgements in the theses (one student acknowledged a foreign research council for funding; another thanked a number of people for their help during the student's stay 'in this country', etc.) and their departments' websites.

Choice of Writing Sample

The master's writing samples were selected by the writers, who were told that the text they chose should be something they had written as part of their theses, in draft form; that it should contain at least six citations (not necessarily to six different sources) and that it should be at least four pages long. In the event that the supervisor had already read and commented on the writing sample, the supervisor's comments would be appreciated. The request for writing in draft form was dictated in part by a hope that ongoing work would be fresher in participants' memories, but also to provide a safeguard for the writers if inappropriate source use came to light during the study. Working with drafts allowed the writers to revise to address any problems.

In the event, six of the nine students supplied recently completed drafts, and five of those six came from parts of the thesis which reviewed research relevant to their topics. The sixth was a bit different; Helen, a student in linguistics from Taiwan, gave me what was essentially an outline of the whole work, with some parts, including a literature review, written in considerable detail, while other parts were sketchier, consisting in some places only of section headings to indicate the intended structure the finished dissertation would have. The other three writing samples were completed works of some sort. Ingrid's was a review of literature on her topic which she had done the previous term as a piece of assessed work and would become a chapter in her thesis. The two civil engineers produced no drafts at all before completing and submitting the theses shortly before the deadline, at which point they gave me the entire works, and I selected samples from relatively citation-dense sections, trying to the extent possible to make the selection consistent with the other writing samples.

I then selected samples from the early chapters of the PhD theses, because those were denser in citations than later ones. To make them similar to the dissertation samples in length, I copied about ten pages from each thesis, sometimes adding an eleventh page to allow the sample to end at a natural section boundary. Before finalizing the choice of writing sample I checked a sample of citations to ensure that at least some of the sources referred to would be available. Apart from those two considerations—density of citations and availability of some of the sources—the pages taken as part of the sample were chosen at random. The selected portions were then photocopied, as were parts of the reference lists, in compliance with fair use restrictions.

The Interviews

Two interviews of approximately one hour in length were conducted with students and one with supervisors. One of the engineering students, Yves, was unavailable for an interview until after he had completed his dissertation, so a single combined interview was arranged. Another student left Britain before being able to schedule a second interview, and responded instead to written questions. Interviews were audiotaped with the consent of the participants and transcribed, and I took notes during and immediately after the interviews.

The first student interview was intended to explore their experience with academic writing and working with sources, and included questions about:

- the student's educational and language background, including previous and current instructions in English, academic writing and the use of sources;
- progress and experiences with working on the dissertation and
- awareness of citation conventions and source use practices.

Interviews were loosely structured around a flexible schedule of topics. Towards the end of the interview students were asked to perform three tasks designed to measure their familiarity with citation conventions: (1) matching terms related to source use with their definitions, (2) identifying instances of quotation and paraphrase in an excerpt from a research article and (3) identifying the stance indicated by reporting verbs.

The purpose of the second interviews was to obtain students' accounts of their source use, and so it took place after analysis of the writing sample had begun. The interview was largely structured around discussion of specific points in the writing sample. Early in each interview I gave the student a copy of the writing sample with a number of passages marked and labelled with a letter for ease of reference. I would then identify a passage and ask the student to comment on it, beginning with general questions and then probing with more specific ones.

In addition to the discussion of specific passages, there were several areas which were covered routinely in all interviews. I asked participants to summarize their supervisors' comments on the writing sample, and to describe how they had prepared the text, from identifying material to read, through the reading and notetaking process to writing. Then, towards the end I asked students to perform two tasks with the writing samples. One was to mark, using two different colours of highlighter pens, the places where they had quoted and the places where they had paraphrased from a source. Then I gave a neutral explanation of the distinction between primary and secondary sources, and asked students to say, for each source cited in their writing samples, which they had consulted and which had been cited through another source. Finally, following Rubin and Rubin, I concluded each interview with the question: 'Now that you have a clearer idea what the research is about, is there anything that I should have asked but didn't?' (1995, p. 137).

The primary purpose of the supervisor interviews was to learn how the students' source use appeared in light of conventional disciplinary practices. The discussion began generally with a request for the supervisor's reaction to the writing sample, and then I progressed to asking specifically about the source use, whether the student had covered the appropriate issues and referred to the appropriate sources for them. The bulk of each interview, though, focused on specific points in the writing samples. As in the second student interviews, I prepared, before each interview, a copy of the writing sample for the supervisor to refer to, with passages labelled for reference. For each passage I intended to ask about, the relevant source was at hand. Again, I began by directing the supervisor's attention to the passage and the source and inviting comment generally, probing with more specific questions if necessary to elicit a response.

Textual Comparison

The purpose of the textual analysis was to see how the sources had been used in the student texts, and that, naturally, required comparing the writing samples with their sources. Doing that depended on three considerations with both theoretical and practical ramifications:

1 it had to be known what sources were used,
2 the sources had to be available for comparison and
3 it had to be possible to infer and support a causal relationship for the similarities between the two texts.

Because these considerations are rather important in understanding how this research was carried out, they will be discussed in some detail here.

Identifying the Sources Used

Since the investigation was not primarily concerned with intentional plagiarism, the only sources used for comparison were those referred to by the students. Nonetheless, there were difficulties involved in identifying which sources were referred to. Reference lists were, of course, available for the PhD writing samples, since they came from completed theses, but in five of the eight theses there were demonstrable inaccuracies in the reference list, some of which—for example, entries missing altogether—were serious enough to make identifying a given source difficult or impossible. The dissertations presented an even greater challenge. Five of the nine had reference lists, which, given that they were still under progress, were even more prone to inaccuracy than the PhD theses, and the other four did not list sources at all, apart from the in-text references. The dissertation writers were very helpful in answering my questions about their sources, but frequently expressed uncertainty about the details. Erden, for example, cited an article as 'Withers, 1991'. When I asked him where the article had appeared, he pulled out a stack of note cards on which he had recorded bibliographic information about his sources, but found four publications by Withers from 1991 and was unsure which of the four he had referred to in his writing sample.

Missing source attribution was often readily apparent, but other, less visible problems could exist unsuspected. To give just two examples, the wrong source could be named in a citation; or the part of the text to which the writer intended a citation to apply might be unclear, creating the impression that no citation appeared for a given point when the writer had meant to supply one, or vice versa. In short, it could not be assumed that the apparent, signalled use of sources corresponded to what the writer had actually done. Indeed, the possible gap between appearance and reality in source use was the principal focus of this investigation. Consequently, determining which sources to compare with the writing samples was a matter of judgement, not certainty, and the sources ultimately used for comparison were not always the ones cited, but the ones which appeared, on balance, to be the actual sources.

The principal criterion used to make those judgements was the similarity between the writing sample and the putative source, with greater similarity permitting greater confidence that the right source was being compared. Some indications could also be gained from the relative accessibility of sources. Thus, in (71a) the source of the quotation appears to be the *Encyclopedia of the Social Sciences*. However, in reading another source—Verma and Beard, 1981—cited elsewhere in the writing sample, I found the same passage from the *Encyclopedia,* and in Verma and Beard it is introduced in the same way as in the student text ('There is some agreement . . .').

72a There is some agreement however, about its general nature. The Encyclopedia of Social Sciences (1934) defines research as:

"The manipulation of things, concepts of symbols for the purpose of generating and to extend, correct or verify knowledge." (p.330)

[SS2]

71b There is some agreement, however, about the general nature of research. A few randomly selected definitions from the literature might provide an answer to what is meant by research.

Encyclopedia of the Social Sciences (1934) offers the following definition:

... manipulation of things, concepts or symbols for the purpose of generalising and to extend, correct or verify knowledge, whether that knowledge aids in the construction of a theory or in the practice of an art.

... (pp. 330–4)
[Verma and Beard, 1981, p. 16]

The primary basis for identifying Verma and Beard as the source is the fact that the student text is more similar to Verma and Beard than to the *Encyclopedia*. However, this conclusion is further supported by the fact that the student's university library, according to its catalogue, only held the *Encyclopedia* at a remote branch, and in a different edition, while the Verma and Beard volume was readily available.

Although some inference is required in identifying the sources actually used, there is a built-in safeguard in that the most serious consequence of identifying the wrong source for comparison would be in using the erroneous comparison as a basis for identifying textual plagiarism. However, using the wrong source for comparison would almost inevitably result in *less* similarity between the two texts, and not more. The result of possible wrong inferences would, therefore, be to make the findings of textual plagiarism more conservative.

The comparison of a source and citing text was done visually, which may be a surprising choice, given the widespread use of electronic plagiarism detection systems. That approach was discarded, though, partly because relatively few of the sources were available electronically, and partly because I wanted to investigate alterations to the language of the sources as well as the similarities that comparison software can turn up.

Part of the analysis involved arriving at a quantitative measure of the similarity between a text and its sources. The following conventions were adopted for identifying words in common between two texts:

- Words which appeared as different word classes in the two texts were not counted in common. So, for example, 'evaluated continuously' and 'evaluation. . . continuous' were not counted as being shared by the student text and its source.

- Different inflections of the same word were counted as being the same. Thus 'went hand in hand' was counted when the source had 'go hand in hand'. In the specific case of verb phrases which consisted of more than one word ('is changed') and which did not occur in the source text in an identical form, all parts of the verb phrase were counted if the change concerned voice, tense or aspect. If a modal verb was present in the student text but not in the source, it was not counted. The rationale behind this decision was that semantic value of modal verbs substantially changes the content and that portion of the verb could appropriately be treated as a new word rather than a repeated one.

- Words which appeared to be misspelled, or spelled according to different conventions (e.g. 'standardised', 'standardized') were counted in common.

- Words appearing in an abbreviated or symbolic form in one text and spelled out fully in another were counted. Thus *B. oleracea* and *Brassica oleracea,* or 23 and twenty-three would be treated as the same word. Sometimes, particularly in the case of the engineering writing samples, it was necessary to consult an informant from the field to understand whether two abbreviations were equivalent.

Importantly, only the language used in the relevant portion of the source was considered in the comparison. That is to say, I did not search all of Bohuon et al. to see if the word 'differ', used by Ingrid, was also used somewhere in their article; it was counted as being in common because it appeared in a contextually related passage in both texts. In cases where students had condensed a source by gathering and joining short phrases across a page or two, discerning the 'relevant portion' was admittedly subjective, but the principle guiding that decision was to search for contextual connections and not to 'cherry-pick'.

In the engineering writing samples the special case of tables, figures and equations arose. Although they differed in important ways from the prose passages of the other writing samples, such features are central elements of engineering writing. It was therefore important to integrate these features into the main body of the data rather than treating them separately, and to accomplish this, the following conventions were adopted. A simple word count was performed on tables and equations, in the same way as it was done for the main body of text; that is, the word count feature of Microsoft Word was used, or if the count was carried out manually, the same criteria used by Word were employed. An important practical consequence of this is that numerical entries in tables were counted as one word each, and equations were counted as one word, unless they spanned more than one line. This procedure resulted in the prose passages appearing disproportionately significant when compared to tables and equations, which are quite dense in their informational content. $E = mc2$, for example, would have been counted as one word according to the conventions applied here, although it could be written out as 'energy is equal to mass multiplied by the square of the speed of light' to create a 14-word sentence. In spite of the imbalance created by this approach, it was selected primarily because it could be applied quite consistently.

Figures were a more difficult case, since they typically consisted of only a few words of caption and key, and so counting only the words and disregarding the graphic representations would skew not only the relevance of the passage to the text, but the degree of similarity between equivalent figures in two works. One solution would have been to treat the figures entirely separately from the other compared passages. However, since they constituted an important element of the engineering sample, segregating the figures would have made it much more difficult to obtain an overview of the main issue—similarity between original and cited form—in the works in that field. I elected instead to include the figures with other passages in the word counts by assigning a nominal number of words to each figure, relative to the amount of space it occupied in the text and the density of information it carried and then assigned a number of words in common on the basis of the similarity it had to the source. Thus a figure which was accorded a nominal 100 words, and had a very high degree of similarity with its source, might be included in the word count as having 80 'words' in common. While this admittedly added an impressionistic element to a category of comparison which was created to provide an objective reference, it was the only solution which allowed all the data from all the writing samples to be compared.

Inferring a Causal Relationship from Similarity

The final area of difficulty that must be confronted in describing the relationship between two texts is that of attributing a causal relationship to observed similarities. That is, if two sources use the same language, is that because the second writer was drawing on the earlier source, or is it coincidence? In some ways this question overlaps with the earlier one of determining which was the source for a passage, but it is not precisely the same question. Identifying a text as a source requires showing that the writer read it and was influenced by its ideas in some ways. Now we must go one step further and show that if there are similarities of language between the two, it is because the newer work was modelled on the older one. What is at issue here is not the probabilistic question of how likely it is that x was the source for y, but the epistemological question of how we can know whether x was the source for y.

This is not a purely theoretical question, because a common defence against plagiarism charges is coincidence, that there are only so many ways to write a given idea, and so there is bound to be similarity between two attempts at expressing the same point. In a plagiarism case, this argument is either accepted or rejected (by a disciplinary body, by an actual jury in some cases or by public opinion) in a legalistic way, based on the preponderance of the evidence, and with regard to whether the facts leave room for reasonable doubt. However, because plagiarism is an act of misconduct, it is taken for granted that the accused will deny guilt, and that denial is largely disregarded. The question observers pose, then, tends to be: 'is there any reasonable doubt that that degree of similarity came about coincidentally?' That, however, brings the question back to probabilities.

Is there any way to avoid the risk of inference and get at the actual nature of source use? This is an important question for the present investigation, which is concerned not so much with the guilt or innocence of an intentionally deceptive plagiarist, but with patchwriting, a source-dependent writing strategy which can only be understood as a process. There are two sources of information which could, in theory, speak to this point, although each presents some difficulties.

The writer can, in principle, know to what extent he or she has been influenced by a source, and if the issue is divorced from plagiarism and wrongdoing, there is no need for the writer to conceal source use strategies in self-defence. But a writer may not be fully aware of the extent to which previous texts have influenced a new one. This is illustrated in an extreme way by the phenomenon of cryptomnesia, source-memory forgetting (e.g. Marsh and Bower, 1993), but with the passing of time any writer can find that the memory of the writing process has faded. So the writer's account, even if it is taken to be entirely candid, may not be entirely accurate, and in establishing the actual origins of a text it may be a useful component but one with limitations.

A second approach would be to set a threshold for the degree of similarity likely to occur between two texts by coincidence, and take the position that above that threshold similarity is unlikely to have occurred by coincidence, and that it is therefore safe to assume a causal relationship for it. However, as discussed in Chapter 4, no rigorous 'plagiarism threshold' exists. There is, therefore, no certain litmus test for plagiarism. The conclusion that the student texts and their sources are indeed related rests on inference, because it must.

Ethical Concerns in Researching a Sensitive Topic

The ethical implications, a legitimate area of concern for any research project, are especially salient when the research involves a sensitive topic (Lee, 1993; Lee and Renzetti, 1993; Rubin and Rubin, 1995) such as plagiarism. Sensitive research topics involve special risks, such as the possibility that incriminating behaviour may be discovered and punished. Any researcher who works with human participants has a duty to them, including obtaining their informed consent, ensuring their privacy and taking steps to anticipate and avoid any harm to them (Fontana and Frey, 1994, p. 372). However, these responsibilities are especially important in research on sensitive topics because the risks are so much higher (Sieber, 1993).

The risks commonly associated with research on a sensitive topic are that the participants or people close to them may be identified; that this may result in confidential or personal information being revealed; that the penalties or stigma which attach to the topic may be brought to bear on participants; that negative attention on the topic would have an impact on all members of the group involved, and on participants as members of that group; and that participants may experience negative feelings ranging from stress to embarrassment or shame at discussing the research topic which is generally not openly addressed (Brannen, 1988; Sieber, 1993).

Three risks merited particular attention in this project. First, I was concerned that students might connect my questions about source use with the issue of plagiarism, and feel embarrassed, under suspicion, or otherwise uncomfortable. Given that I had made contact with the students through their supervisors, this could create a backlash not only for me and my research, but for the student–teacher relationship as well. Secondly, there was the risk that the close examination of the students' writing which would take place in the interviews might cause supervisors to realize that the writing samples contained instances of source use which required revision. Given the time pressures every thesis writer labours under, the possibility of being told to rewrite significant proportions of the work would have been no minor matter. Finally, there was the risk that the writing samples might be judged—either by the supervisors, during the study, or later and by other parties, if the students' privacy were breached—to contain plagiarism. This could have a number of consequences, including disciplinary action being taken against a participant.

The research methods were designed to minimize these risks. Participants' informed consent was obtained by providing them with a detailed information sheet, written in language which was designed to be as accessible as possible, and I ended the information sheet, and began and ended each interview, with an invitation to the participants to ask questions. The information sheet mentioned the risk that a close examination of their writing might lead to them and/or the supervisors feeling that additional work was necessary, and by asking for writing samples which were drafts I hoped that any problems identified could be fixed in the normal revision process.

The possible risks of a plagiarism accusation could not be addressed directly since, for several reasons, it seemed ill-advised to raise the issue of plagiarism at all. This was in part to avoid the risk of directing participants' responses, and failing to hear their wider accounts, but also to avoid embarrassment or discomfort. In addition, using the label 'plagiarism' carried a risk that participants might have difficulty relating the term to their own experiences (Brannen, 1988) (although an opposing view is registered by Fielding, 1993, who argues that a researcher may be both more honest and more likely to obtain rich results by acknowledging his or her view when participants behave in a way which is generally regarded in a negative light).

Similarly, any question about writing behaviour which could be taken as an implied criticism—for instance, the questions about primary and secondary source use—was asked in such a way as to err on the friendly, rather than the accusatory, side of neutral. I also made a point of mentioning that my research was an investigation of how academic writing is done in various disciplines. By positioning myself as a disciplinary outsider, I tried to make it clear that my role in the interviews was not that of judge. For all these reasons, the word 'plagiarism' or other euphemisms for it, such as 'borrowing', were not used, unless the student first mentioned 'plagiarism', and throughout the interviews I attempted to give the impression of being approving rather than condemning or judgemental (Taylor and Bogdan, 1998, p. 100).

Since the most serious risk in terms of consequences to the students was that plagiarism might be identified in their writing by someone reading about my research, an extremely important concern was that of protecting the identity of participants, which I did by giving them pseudonyms, and not naming their universities or departments. I took the same precautions to protect the privacy of the PhD students, to avoid a situation in which their identities could be revealed. I did not, however, feel the same responsibility to protect them that I perceived with regard to the dissertation writers, because the PhD students were not themselves participants in my research; I simply consulted their completed theses, which were available to anyone.

A final point to be made in mitigation of the risks is that involvement in a research project can involve some benefits to the participants. Talking through experiences may provide a new perspective on them (Taylor and Bogdan, 1998, p. 98). The interviewees may also find the talk enjoyable since it will be, by definition, on a topic of interest to them (Kvale, 1996, p. 36). If the topic is stressful, as sensitive issues frequently are, the participant may find the process cathartic (Brannen, 1988; Lee and Renzetti, 1993, p. 9). The comments of the student participants seemed to indicate that many of them found the interview process interesting and beneficial to some extent.

One risk which I failed to foresee, though, was that the supervisors would experience the same feelings of embarrassment I had hoped to spare the students. That was, however, precisely what happened. Some reported feeling 'caught out', expressing a belief that they should have been able to detect problematic source use when reading the samples prior to the interview. In one interview, when the tape had been turned off and I was taking my leave, the supervisor confided that she felt that she should have picked up on those issues. She then made a semi-joking reference to needing to go home and have a stiff drink.

It is clear, though, that those costs were associated with benefits to the participants. Although he was one of the supervisors who expressed discomfort at discovering source-dependent writing in his students' work, Dr Morse said:

> . . . it's made me more aware of the problem, which is good; it's a positive element. It might and certainly it might make me more aware, it has made me more aware that they probably do need much more explicit instruction in conventions, and more training in that, so that's all a good thing.

He held the view, which was part of the initial assumption of the research, that if a problem is there to be found, revealing it can be uncomfortable but may be beneficial in the long run.

References

Abasi, A. R., Akbari, N., & Graves, B. (2006). Discourse appropriation, construction of identities and the complex issue of plagiarism: ESL students writing in graduate school. *Journal of Second Language Writing, 15,* 102–117.

Acker, S., Hill, T., & Black, E. (1994). Thesis supervision in the social sciences: Managed or negotiated? *Higher Education, 28,* 483–498.

Alexander, J. D. (1988). Lectures: The ethics of borrowing. *College Teaching, 36,* 21–24.

Allen, B. (1997). Referring to schools of thought: An example of symbolic citations. *Social Studies of Science, 27,* 937–949.

American Psychological Association. (2001). *Publication manual of the American Psychological Association.* Washington, DC: American Psychological Association.

Anderson, J. (1998). *Plagiarism, copyright violation and other thefts of intellectual property: An annotated bibliography with a lengthy introduction.* Jefferson, NC: McFarland.

Angélil-Carter, S. (2000). *Stolen language? Plagiarism in writing.* London: Longman.

Austin, M.J., & Brown, L. D. (1999). Internet plagiarism: Developing strategies to curb student academic dishonesty. *The Internet and Higher Education, 2,* 21–33.

Ballard, B., & Clanchy, J. (1991). Assessment by misconception: Cultural influences and intellectual traditions. In L Hamp-Lyons (Ed.), *Assessing writing in academic contexts* (pp. 19–35). Norwood, NJ: Ablex.

Barks, D., & Watts, P. (2001). Textual borrowing strategies for graduate-level ESL writers. In D. Belcher & A. Hirvela (Eds.), *Linking literacies: Perspectives on L2 reading-writing connections* (pp. 246–267). Ann Arbor, MI: University of Michigan Press.

Baron, N. (2000). *Alphabet to email: How written English evolved and where it's heading.* London: Routledge.

Baty, P. (2004). Plagiarist student to sue university. *Times Online.* Retrieved 19 January 2006 from http://www.timesonline.co.uk/article/0,,3561-1126250,00.html.

Bazerman, C. (1984). Modern evolution of the experimental report in physics: Spectroscopic articles in *Physical Review,* 1893–1980. *Social Studies of Science, 14,* 163–196.

Becher, T., & Trowler, P. (2001). *Academic tribes and territories: Intellectual enquiry and the culture of disciplines* (2nd ed.). Philadelphia, PA: Open University Press.

Belcher, D. (1994). The apprenticeship approach to advanced academic literacy: Graduate students and their mentors. *English for Specific Purposes, 13,* 23–34.

Belcher, D. (1997). An argument for nonadversarial argumentation: On the relevance of the feminist critique of academic discourse to L2 writing pedagogy. *Journal of Second Language Writing, 6,* 1–21.

Belcher, D. (2001). Cyberdiscourse, evolving notions of authorship, and the teaching of writing. In M. Hewings (Ed.), *Academic writing in context: Implications and applications* (pp. 140–149). Birmingham: University of Birmingham Press.

Berkenkotter, C., Huckin, T. N., & Ackerman, J. (1995 [1988]). Conventions, conversations, and the writer: An apprenticeship tale of a doctoral student. In C. Berkenkotter & T.N. Huckin (Eds.), *Genre knowledge in disciplinary communication: Cognition/culture/power* (pp. 117–144). Hillsdale, NJ: Erlbaum.

Berkenkotter, C., & Huckin, T. (1995). *Genre knowledge in disciplinary communication: Cognition/culture/power.* Hillsdale, NJ: Lawrence Erlbaum.

Best, R., Ribbins, P., Jarvis, C., & Oddy, D. (1983). *Education and care.* London: Heinemann.

Betts, D. D. (1992). Retraction of an article published in the *Canadian Journal of Physics. Canadian Journal of Physics, 70,* 289.

Biber, D., Johansson, S., Leech, G., Conrad, S., & Finegan., E. (1999). *Longman grammar of spoken and written English.* Harlow, UK: Longman.

Biggs, J. B. (1996). Enhancing teaching through constructive alignment. *Higher Education, 32,* 347–364.

Biglan, A. (1973a). The characteristics of subject matter in different academic areas. *Journal of Applied Psychology, 57,* 195–203.

Biglan, A. (1973b). Relationships between subject matter characteristics and the structure of and output of university departments. *Journal of Applied Psychology, 57,* 204–213.

Bjerrum, L. (1967). Engineering geology of Norwegian normally-consolidated marine clays as related to settlements of buildings. *Géotechnique, 17,* 81–118.

Black, M. (1962). *Models and metaphors: Studies in language and philosophy.* Ithaca, NY: Cornell University Press.

Bloch, J. (2001). Plagiarism and the ESL student: From printed to electronic texts. In D. Belcher & A. Hirvela (Eds.), *Linking literacies:*

Perspectives on L2 reading-writing connections (pp. 209–228). Ann Arbor, MI: University of Michigan Press.

Bloch, J., & Chi, L. (1995). A comparison of the use of citations in Chinese and English academic discourse. In D. Belcher & G. Braine (Eds.), *Academic writing in a second language: Essays on research and pedagogy* (pp. 231–274). Norwood, NJ: Ablex.

Bowden, D. (1996). Plagiarism. *English Journal, 85*(4), 82–84.

Braine, G. (1995). Writing in the natural sciences and engineering. In D. Belcher & G. Braine (Eds.), *Academic writing in a second language: Essays on research and pedagogy* (pp. 113–134). Norwood, NJ: Ablex.

Brannen, J. (1988). The study of sensitive subjects. *Sociological Review, 36,* 552–563.

Brenner, R. P., Nutalaya, P., Chilingarian, G. V., & Robertson, J. O. (1981). Engineering geology of soft clay. In E. W. Brand & R. P. Brenner (Eds.), *Soft clay engineering* (pp. 159–238). Amsterdam: Elsevier.

Brogan, K. M., & Brogan, J. D. (1983). *Yet another ethical problem in technical writing* (ERIC Document Reproduction Service No. ED 229 782).

Broughton, G., Brumfit, C., Flavell, R., Hill, P., & Pincas, A. (1978). *Teaching English as a foreign language*. London: Routledge & Kegan Paul.

Buranen, L. (1999). 'But I *wasn't* cheating': Plagiarism and cross-cultural mythology. In L. Buranen & A. M. Roy (Eds.), *Perspectives on plagiarism and intellectual property in a postmodern world* (pp. 63–74). Albany, NY: State University of New York Press.

Burton, R. E., & Kebler, R.W. (1960). The 'half-life' of some scientific and technical literatures. *American Documentation, 11,* 18–22.

Burtonwood, N. (1986). *The culture concept in educational studies.* Windsor: NFER-Nelson.

Cammish, N.K. (1997). Through a glass darkly: Problems of studying at advanced level through the medium of English. In D. McNamara & R. Harris (Eds.), *Overseas students in higher education: Issues in teaching and learning* (pp. 143–155). London: Routledge.

Campbell, C. (1990). Writing with others' words: Using background reading text in academic compositions. In B. Kroll (Ed.), *Second language writing* (pp. 211–230). Cambridge: Cambridge University Press.

Chandrasegaran, A. (2000). Cultures in contact in academic writing: Students' perceptions of plagiarism. *Asian Journal of English Language Teaching, 10,* 91–113.

Chandrasoma, R., Thompson, C., & Pennycook, A. (2004). Beyond plagiarism: Transgressive and nontransgressive intertextuality. *Journal of Language, Identity and Education, 3,* 171–193.

Charles, M. (2006a). Phraseological patterns in reporting clauses used in citation: A corpus-based study of theses in two disciplines. *English for Specific Purposes, 25,* 310–331.
Charles, M. (2006b). The construction of stance in reporting clauses: A cross-disciplinary study of theses. *Applied Linguistics, 27,* 492–518.
Concise Oxford English Dictionary. (2004). (11th ed.). Oxford: Oxford University Press.
Connor, U. M., & Kramer, M. G. (1995). Writing from sources: Case studies of graduate students in business management. In D. Belcher & G. Braine (Eds.), *Academic writing in a second language: Essays on research and pedagogy* (pp. 155–182). Norwood, NJ: Ablex.
Cook, G. (1994). Repetition and learning by heart: An aspect of intimate discourse, and its implications. *ELT Journal, 48,* 133–141.
Cooper, D. E. (1986). *Metaphor.* Oxford: Blackwell.
Cosgrove, S. (1989). In praise of plagiarism. *New Statesman & Society, 2*(65), 38–39.
Coulthard, M. (2004). Author identification, idiolect, and linguistic uniqueness. *Applied Linguistics, 25,* 431–447.
Cozzens, S. E. (1982). Split citation identity: A case study from economics. *Journal of the American Society for Information Science, 33,* 233–236.
Cozzens, S. E. (1985). Comparing the sciences: Citation context analysis of papers from neuropharmacology and the sociology of science. *Social Studies of Science, 15,* 127–153.
Crocker, J., & Shaw, P. (2002). Research student and supervisor evaluation of intertextuality practices. *Hermes, 28,* 39–58.
Cronin, B. (1981). The need for a theory of citing. *Journal of Documentation, 37,* 16–24.
Cunningsworth, A. (1995). *Choosing your coursebook.* Oxford: Heinemann.
Currie, P. (1998). Staying out of trouble: Apparent plagiarism and academic survival. *Journal of Second Language Writing, 7,* 1–18.
Damich, E. J. (1987, 27 September). Serious and shocking. *New York Times,* pp. 4, 22.
Datta, A., Ganesan, K., & Natarajan, K. (1989). Current trends in *Candida albicans* research. *Advances in Microbial Physiology, 30,* 53–88.
Deckert, G. D. (1993). Perspectives on plagiarism from ESL students in Hong Kong. *Journal of Second Language Writing, 2,* 131–148.
DeGroot, G. (2000, 22 February). Cheats are scaring us stiff. *Guardian Education Supplement,* p. 4H.
Dionne, E. J. (1987a, 17 September). Biden was accused of plagiarism in law school. *New York Times,* p. A1.
Dionne, E. J. (1987b, 24 September). Biden withdraws bid for President in wake of furor. *New York Times,* p. A1.

Dionne, E. J. (1987c, 18 September). Biden admits plagiarism in school but says it was not 'malevolent'. *New York Times*, p. A1.
Dionne, E. J. (1987d, 22 September). Biden admits errors and criticizes latest report. *New York Times*, p. A26.
Dionne, E. J. (1987e, 20 September). The nation: Tailoring rhetoric of others for candidates' new clothes. *New York Times*, pp. 4–5.
Dong, Y. R. (1996). Learning how to use citations for knowledge transformation: Non-native doctoral students' dissertation writing in science. *Research in the Teaching of English, 30,* 428–457.
Dong, Y. R. (1998). Non-native graduate students' thesis/dissertation writing in science: Self-reports by students and their advisors from two US institutions. *English for Specific Purposes, 17,* 369–390.
Dowd, M. (1987, 12 September). Biden's debate finale: An echo from abroad. *New York Times*, p. A1.
Dryden, L. M. (1999). A distant mirror or through the looking glass? Plagiarism and intellectual property in Japanese education. In L. Buranen & A. M. Roy (Eds.), *Perspectives on plagiarism and intellectual property in a postmodern world* (pp. 74–85). Albany, NY: State University of New York Press.
Dubois, B. L. (1988). Citation in biomedical journal articles. *English for Specific Purposes, 7,* 181–193.
Dysthe, O. (2002). Professors as mediators of academic text cultures: An interview study with advisors and master's degree students in three disciplines in a Norwegian university. *Written Communication, 19,* 493–544.
Erman, B., & Warren, B. (2000). The idiom principle and the open choice principle. *Text, 20,* 29–62.
Errey, L. (2002). Plagiarism: Something fishy . . . or just a fish out of water? *Teaching Forum, 50,* 17–20.
Faure, O., Diemer, F., Moja, S., & Jullien, F. (1998). Mannitol and thidiazuron improve *in vitro* shoot regeneration from spearmint and peppermint leaf disks. *Plant Cell, Tissue and Organ Culture, 52,* 209–212.
Fielding, N. (1993). Mediating the message: Affinity and hostility. In C. M. Renzetti & R. M. Lee (Eds.), *Researching sensitive topics* (pp. 146–159). Newbury Park, CA: Sage.
Flower, L. (1979). Writer-based prose: A cognitive basis for problems in writing. *College English, 41,* 19–37.
Flowerdew, J. (2000). Discourse community, legitimate peripheral participation, and the non-native-English-speaking scholar. *TESOL Quarterly, 34,* 127–150.
Flowerdew, J., & Li, Y. (2007). Language re-use among Chinese apprentice scientists writing for publication. *Applied Linguistics, 28,* 440–465.

Fontana, A., & Frey, J. (1994). Interviewing: The art of science. In N. K. Denzin & Y. S. Lincoln (Eds.), *Handbook of qualitative research* (pp. 361–376). Thousand Oaks, CA: Sage.

Force, P., & Jullien, D. (1988). Renaud Camus. *Yale French Studies Special Issue*, 285–290.

Friedman, E. G. (1989, Fall). 'Now eat your mind': An introduction to the works of Kathy Acker. *The Review of Contemporary Fiction, 9,* 37–49.

Gardner, H. (1995). *Leading minds: An anatomy of leadership.* London: HarperCollins.

Garrow, D. J. (1991). King's plagiarism: Imitation, insecurity, and transformation. *The Journal of American History, 78,* 86–92.

Geisler, C. (1991). Toward a sociocognitive model of literacy: Constructing mental models in a philosophical conversation. In C. Bazerman & J. Paradis (Eds.), *Textual dynamics of the professions: Historical and contemporary studies of writing in professional communities* (pp. 171–190). Madison, WI: University of Wisconsin Press.

Giamatti, A. B. (1987, 27 September). A form of theft. Letter to the *New York Times,* p. 4, 22.

Gibaldi, J. (2003). *MLA handbook for writers of research papers* (6th ed.). New York: MLA.

Gilbert, N. (1977). Referencing as persuasion. *Social Studies of Science, 7,* 113–122.

Glod, M. (2006, 22 September). Students rebel against database designed to thwart plagiarists. *Washington Post.* Retrieved 29 September 2007 from http://www.washingtonpost.com/wpdyn/content/ article/2006/09/21/AR2006092101800_pf.html

Glod, M. (2007, 29 March). McLean students sue anti-cheating service: Plaintiffs say company's database of term papers, essays violates copyright laws. *Washington Post.* Retrieved 29 September 2007 from http://www.washingtonpost.com/wp-dyn/content/article/2007/03/28/AR2007032802038.html

Gosden, H. (1996). Verbal reports of Japanese novices' research writing practices in English. *Journal of Second Language Writing, 5,* 109–128.

Grimmett, P. P., & Crehan, E. P. (1992). The nature of collegiality in teacher development. In M. Fullan & A. Hargreaves (Eds.), *Teacher development and educational change* (pp. 56–85). London: Falmer Press.

Groom, N. (2000). Attribution and averral revisited: Three perspectives on manifest intertextuality in academic writing. In P. Thompson (Ed.), *Patterns and perspectives: Insights into EAP writing practice* (pp. 14–25). Reading, UK: Center for Applied Language Studies.

Gunnarsson, H. (2005, 18 October). Rosenbergs forskning granskas inte. *Dagens Nyheter.* Retrieved 29 June 2007 from http://www.dn.se/DNet/road/Classic/article/0/jsp/print.jsp?&a=475918.
Ha, P. L. (2006). Plagiarism and overseas students: Stereotypes again? *ELT Journal, 60,* 76–78.
Halbert, D. (1999). Poaching and plagiarizing: Property, plagiarism and feminist futures. In L. Buranen & A. M. Roy (Eds.), *Perspectives on plagiarism and intellectual property in a postmodern world* (pp. 111–120). Albany, NY: State University of New York Press.
Hanania, E., & Akhtar, K. (1985). Verb form and rhetorical function in science writing: A study of MS theses in biology, chemistry and physics. *ESP Journal, 4,* 49–58.
Harrison, D. (2005, 7 October). Vi professorer gör alla som Fi–Tiina. *Expressen.* Retrieved 29 June 2007 from http://www.expressen.se/debatt/1.259917.
Harwood, N. (2008). Citers' use of citees' names: Findings from a qualitative interview-based study. *Journal of the American Society for Information Science and Technology.*
Harwood, N. (2004). Citation analysis: A multidisciplinary perspective on academic literacy. In M. Baynham, A. Deignan, & G. White (Eds.), *Applied linguistics at the interface* (pp. 79–89). London: BAAL and Equinox.
Hayes, N., & Introna, L. D. (2005). Cultural values, plagiarism, and fairness: When plagiarism gets in the way of learning. *Ethics and Behavior, 15*(3), 213–231.
Hayes, N., & Introna, L. D (2006). Systems for the production of plagiarists? The implications arising from the use of plagiarism detection systems in UK universities for Asian learners. *Journal of Academic Ethics, 3,* 55–73.
Hewings, M., & Houghton, D. (1992). Making economics more accessible: A study of the process of rewriting an economics text for a wider readership. In B.-L. Gunnarsson, P. Linell, & B. Nordberg (Eds.), *Text and talk in professional contexts: Selected papers from the international conference 'Discourse and the professions'* (pp. 105–123). Uppsala, Sweden: Association of Applied Linguistics.
Higham, J. (1991). Habits of the cloth and standards of the academy. *The Journal of American History, 78,* 106–110.
Howard, R. M. (1995). Plagiarisms, authorships, and the academic death penalty. *College English, 57,* 788–805.
Howard, R. M. (1999). *Standing in the shadow of giants.* Stamford, CT: Ablex.
Howard, R. M. (2001, 17 March). *Plagiarism: What should a teacher do?* Paper presented at the Conference on College Composition and Communication, Denver, Colorado. Retrieved 26 May 2002 from http://wrthoward.syr.edu/Papers/CCCC2001.html

Howard, R. M. (2007, 5–7 September). Paper presented at the International Students, Academic Writing and Plagiarism Conference, Lancaster University.
Hull, G., & Rose, M. (1989). Rethinking remediation: Toward a social-cognitive understanding of problematic reading and writing. *Written Communication, 6,* 139–154.
Hunston, S. (1995). A corpus study of some English verbs of attribution. *Functions of Language, 2*(2), 133–158.
Hyland, K. (1999). Academic attribution: Citation and the construction of knowledge. *Applied Linguistics, 20,* 341–367.
Hyland, K. (2000). *Disciplinary discourses: Social interactions in academic writing.* Harlow, Essex: Longman.
Hyland, K. (2003). Self-citation and self-reference: Credibility and promotion in academic publication. *Journal of the American Society for Information Science and Technology, 54,* 251–259.
Introna, L., Hayes, N., Whitley, E., & Timm, A. (2007, 5–7 September). *On the limitations of electronic detection software.* Paper presented at the International Students, Academic Writing and Plagiarism Conference, Lancaster University, Lancaster, UK.
Ivanič, R. (1998). *Writing and identity: The discoursal construction of identity in academic writing.* Amsterdam and Philadelphia: John Benjamins.
Jacoby, S. (1987). References to other researchers in literary research articles. *ELR Journal, 1,* 33–78.
Kantz, M. (1990). Helping students use textual sources persuasively. *College English, 52,* 74–91.
Kaplan, N. (1965). The norms of citation behavior: Prolegomena to the footnote. *American Documentation, 16,* 179–184.
Kennard, W. C., Slocum, M. K., Figdore, S. S., & Osborn, T. C. (1994). Genetic analysis of morphological variation in *Brassica oleracea* using molecular markers. *Theoretical and Applied Genetics, 87,* 721–732.
Kirkland, M. R., & Saunders, M. A. P. (1991). Maximizing student performance in summary writing: Managing cognitive load. *TESOL Quarterly, 25,* 105–121.
Klein, D. F. (1993). Should the government assure scientific integrity? *Academic Medicine, 68,* S56–S59.
Kolich, A. (1983). Plagiarism: The worm of reason. *College English, 45,* 141–148.
Krase, E. (2007). 'Maybe the communication between us was not enough': Inside a dysfunctional advisor/L2 advisee relationship. *Journal of English for Academic Purposes, 6,* 55–70.
Kroll, B. M. (1988). How college freshmen view plagiarism. *Written Communication, 5,* 203–221.
Kvale, S. (1996). *InterViews: An introduction to qualitative research interviewing.* Thousand Oaks, CA: Sage.

Lagercrantz, U., Putterill, J., Coupland, G., & Lydiate, D. (1996). Comparative mapping in *Arabidopsis* and *Brassica*, fine scale genome collinearity and congruence of genes controlling flowering time. *The Plant Journal, 9,* 13–20.

Lakoff, G., & Johnson, M. (1980). *Metaphors we live by.* Chicago and London: University of Chicago Press.

Larochelle, G. (1999). From Kant to Foucault: What remains of the author in postmodernism. In L. Buranen & A. M. Roy (Eds.), *Perspectives on plagiarism and intellectual property in a postmodern world* (pp. 121–130). Albany, NY: State University of New York Press.

Lave, J., & Wenger, E. (1991). *Situated learning: Legitimate peripheral participation.* Cambridge: Cambridge University Press.

Leatherman, C. (1999). At Texas A&M, conflicting charges of misconduct tear a program apart. *Chronicle of Higher Education, 46*(11), A18–A20.

Lee, R. (1993). *Doing research on sensitive topics.* London: Sage.

Lee, R. M., & Renzetti, C. M. (1993). The problems of researching sensitive topics: An overview and introduction. In C. M. Renzetti & R. M. Lee (Eds.), *Researching sensitive topics* (pp. 3–13). Newbury Park, CA: Sage.

Leki, I. (1995). Coping strategies of ESL students in writing tasks across the curriculum. *TESOL Quarterly, 29,* 235–260.

Levelt, W. J. M. (1989). *Speaking: From intention to articulation.* Cambridge, MA: MIT Press.

Lipetz, B.-A. (1965). Improvement of the selectivity of citation indexes to science literature through inclusion of citation relationship indicators. *American Documentation, 16,* 81–90.

Liu, D. (2005). Plagiarism in ESOL students: Is cultural conditioning truly the major culprit? *ELT Journal, 59,* 234–241.

LoCastro, V., & Masuko, M. (2002). Plagiarism and academic writing of learners of English. *Hermes Journal of Linguistics, 28,* 11–33.

Lovell, K., & Lawson, K. S. (1970). *Understanding research in education.* London: University of London Press.

Maher, P., & Best, R. (1985). Preparation and support for pastoral care: A survey of current provision. In P. Lang & M. Marland (Eds.), *New directions in pastoral care.* Oxford: Blackwell.

Marsh, R. L., & Bower, G. H. (1993). Eliciting cryptomnesia: Unconscious plagiarism in a puzzle task. *Journal of Experimental Psychology, Learning, Memory and Cognition, 19,* 673–688.

Martin, R. G. (1971). Plagiarism and originality: Some remedies. *English Journal, 60,* 621–625, 628.

Martin Luther King, Jr., Papers Project. (1991). The student papers of Martin Luther King, Jr.: A summary statement on research. *The Journal of American History, 78,* 23–40.

Martin Luther King, Jr., Papers Project at Stanford University. Retrieved 29 May 2002 from http://www.stanford.edu/group/King/

Matalene, C. (1985). Contrastive rhetoric: An American writing teacher in China. *College English, 47,* 789–807.

May, C. D. (1987, 21 September). Washington talk: Political speechmaking, Biden and the annals of raised eyebrows. *New York Times,* p. B8.

McClanahan, K. (2005). *Working through plagiarism and patchwriting: Three L2 writers navigating intertextual worlds.* Unpublished Master's paper, University of Hawai'i at Manoa.

McCracken, E. (1991). Metaplagiarism and the critic's role as detective: Ricardo Piglia's reinvention of Roberto Arlt. *PMLA, 106*(5), 1071–1082.

McKnight, G. D. (1998). *The last crusade: Martin Luther King, Jr., the FBI, and the poor people's campaign.* Boulder, CO: Westview Press.

Meislin, R. J. (1987, 18 September). In hindsight, Biden's law teacher sees offense as minor. *New York Times,* p. A23.

Midgely, S. (2000, 30 May). No copying! *Guardian Education.*

Miller, K. D. (1990). Composing Martin Luther King, Jr. *PMLA, 105*(1), 70–82.

Miller, K. D. (1991). Martin Luther King, Jr., and the Black folk pulpit. *The Journal of American History, 78,* 120–123.

Moravcsik, M. J., & Murugesan, P. (1975). Some results on the function and quality of citations. *Social Studies of Science, 5,* 86–92.

Murphy, R. (1990). Anorexia: The cheating disorder. *College English, 52,* 898–903.

Murray, D. E. (1992). Collaborative writing as a literacy event: Implications for ESL instruction. In D. Nunan (Ed.). *Collaborative language learning and teaching* (pp. 100–117). Cambridge: Cambridge University Press.

Myers, G. (1992). 'In this paper we report . . .': Speech acts and scientific facts. *Journal of Pragmatics, 17,* 295–313.

Nienhuis, T. (1989). The quick fix: Curing plagiarism with a notetaking exercise. *College Teaching, 37*(3), 100.

Nunan, D. (1995). *Language teaching methodology: A textbook for teachers.* Hemel Hempstead: Phoenix.

Nunberg, G. (2005, 1 February). 'The Importance of grammar'. *Fresh Air.* Retrieved 22 July 2007 from http://www.npr.org/templates/story/story.php?storyId=4473683

Nunberg, G. (2006). *Talking right: How conservatives turned liberalism into a tax-raising, latte-drinking, sushi-eating, Volvo-driving, New York Times-reading, body-piercing, Hollywood-loving, left-wing freak show.* New York: Public Affairs.

Oakley, A. (1981). Interviewing women: A contradiction in terms. In H. Roberts (Ed.), *Doing feminist research* (pp. 30–61). London: Routledge.

Palmer, L. R. (1954). *The Latin language.* London: Faber & Faber.

Pecorari, D. (2001). Plagiarism and international students: How the English-speaking university responds. In D. Belcher & A. Hirvela (Eds.), *Linking literacies: Perspectives on L2 reading-writing connections* (pp. 229–245). Ann Arbor, MI: University of Michigan Press.

Pecorari, D. (2003). Good and original: Plagiarism and patchwriting in academic second-language writing. *Journal of Second Language Writing, 12,* 317–345.

Pecorari, D. (2006). Visible and occluded citation features in postgraduate second-language writing. *English for Specific Purposes, 25,* 4–29.

Pennycook, A. (1994) The complex contexts of plagiarism: A response to Deckert. *Journal of Second Language Writing, 3,* 277– 284.

Pennycook, A. (1996). Borrowing others' words: Text, ownership, memory and plagiarism. *TESOL Quarterly, 30,* 201–230.

Petrić, B. (2004). A pedagogical perspective on plagiarism. *NovELTy, 11*(1), 4–18.

Petrić, B. (2007). Rhetorical functions of citations in high and low rated master's theses. *Journal of English for Academic Purposes, 6,* 238–253.

Pickard, V. (1995). Citing previous writers: What can we say instead of 'say'? *Hong Kong Papers in Linguistics and Language Teaching, 18,* 89–102.

'Plagiarising student sues university for negligence'. (2004, 27 May). *Guardian Unlimited.* Retrieved 18 January 2007 from http://education.guardian.co.uk/print/0,,4934062-108229,00.html.

Popham, J. W. (1988). *Educational evaluation* (2nd ed.). Englewood Cliffs, NJ: Prentice Hall.

Porter, B. (2000, 7 March). Take note. *Guardian Education,* 12–13.

Price, D. J. de S. (1965). Networks of scientific papers. *Science, 149,* 510–515.

Prior, P.A. (1998). *Writing/disciplinarity: A sociohistoric account of literate activity in the academy.* Mahwah, NJ: Erlbaum.

Pulgram, E. (1958). *The tongues of Italy: Prehistory and history.* Cambridge, MA: Harvard University Press.

Pyle, D. W., & Sayers, T. A. (1980). A BEd course for serving teachers: An evaluation of the first year. *British Journal of Inservice Education, 7,* 10–37.

Ragen, B. A. (1987, 25 September). A lesson of Biden's plagiarism. *New York Times,* p. A39.

Raines, H. (1987, 9 June). Ballots, ballyhoo and the British way. *New York Times*, p. A3.
Ramsay, L. D., Jennings, D. E., Bohuon, E. J. R., Arthur, A. E., Lydiate, D. J., Kearsey, M. J., et al. (1996). The construction of a substitution library of recombinant backcross lines in *Brassica oleracea* for the precision of mapping quantitative trait loci. *Genome, 39,* 558–567.
Randall, M. (1990). Le présupposé d'originalité et l'art du plagiat: Lecture pragmatique. *Voix et Images, 44,* 196–208.
Randall, M. (1991). Appropriate(d) discourse: Plagiarism and decolonialization. *New Literary History, 22,* 525–541.
Reagon, B. J. (1991). 'Nobody knows the trouble I see'; or 'by and by I'm gonna lay down my heavy load'. *The Journal of American History, 78,* 111–119.
Rheem, D. L. (1987, 25 September). Press glare versus bosses in screening candidates. *Christian Science Monitor.*
Richards, R. T. (1988). Thesis/dissertation writing for EFL students: An ESP course design. *English for Specific Purposes, 7,* 171–180.
Rinnert, C., & Kobayashi, H. (2005). Borrowing words and ideas: Insights from Japanese L1 writers. *Journal of Asian Pacific Communication, 15*(1), 31–56.
Roig, M. (1997). Can undergraduate students determine whether a text has been plagiarized? *Psychological Record, 47,* 113–122.
Roig, M. (2001). Plagiarism and paraphrasing criteria of college and university professors. *Ethics and Behavior, 11,* 307–323.
Rubin, H. J., & Rubin, I. S. (1995). *Qualitative interviewing: The art of hearing data.* Thousand Oaks, CA: Sage.
Safire, W. (1987, 27 September). No heavy lifting. *New York Times Magazine,* p. 12.
Salager-Meyer, F. (1999). Referential behavior in scientific writing: A diachronic study (1810–1995). *English for Specific Purposes, 18,* 279–305.
San Miguel, C., & Nelson, C. D. (2007). Key writing challenges of practice-based doctorates. *Journal of English for Academic Purposes, 6,* 71–86.
Sapp, D. A. (2002). Towards an international and intercultural understanding of plagiarism and academic dishonesty in composition: Reflections from the People's Republic of China. *Issues in Writing, 13,* 58–79.
Sciolino, M. (1989, Fall). Confessions of a kleptoparasite. *The Review of Contemporary Fiction, 9,* 63–67.
Sciolino, M. (1990). Kathy Acker and the postmodern subject of feminism. *College English, 52,* 437–445.
Scollon, R. (1994). As a matter of fact: The changing ideology of authorship and responsibility in discourse. *World Englishes, 13,* 33–46.

Scollon, R. (1995). Plagiarism and ideology: Identity in intercultural discourse. *Language in Society, 24,* 1–28.
Shadish, W. R., Tolliver, D., Gray, M., & Sen Gupta, S. K. (1995). Author judgements about works they cite: Three studies from psychology journals. *Social Studies of Science, 25,* 477–498.
Shaw, P. (1991). Science research students' composing processes. *English for Specific Purposes, 10,* 189–206.
Shaw, P. (1992). Reasons for the correlation of voice, tense and sentence function in reporting verbs. *Applied Linguistics, 13,* 302–319.
Sherman, J. (1992). Your own thoughts in your own words. *ELT Journal, 46,* 190–198.
Shi, L. (2004). Textual borrowing in second-language writing. *Written Communication, 21,* 171–200.
Shi, L. (2006). Cultural backgrounds and textual appropriation. *Language Awareness, 15,* 264–282.
Shibata, N., Kajikawa, Y., & Matsushima, K. (2007). Topological analysis of citation networks to discover the future core articles. *Journal of the American Society for Information Science and Technology, 58,* 872–882.
Sieber, J. E. (1993) The ethics and politics of sensitive research. In C. M. Renzetti & R. M. Lee (Eds.), *Researching sensitive topics* (pp. 14–26). Newbury Park, CA: Sage.
Simmons, S. C. (1999). Competing notions of authorship: A historical look at students and textbooks on plagiarism and cheating. In L. Buranen & A. M. Roy (Eds.), *Perspectives on plagiarism and intellectual property in a postmodern world* (pp. 41–51). Albany, NY: State University of New York Press.
Sinclair, J. M. (1986). Fictional worlds. In M. Coulthard (Ed.), *Talking about text* (pp. 43–60). Birmingham: University of Birmingham.
Sinclair, J. M. (1987). Mirror for a text. *MS,* University of Birmingham.
Small, H. G. (1974). Multiple citation patterns in scientific literature: The circle and hill models. *Information Storage and Retrieval, 10,* 393–402.
Small, H. G. (1977). A co-citation model of a scientific specialty: A longitudinal study of collagen research. *Social Studies of Science, 7,* 139–166.
Small, H. G. (1978). Cited documents as concept symbols. *Social Studies of Science, 8,* 327–340.
Small, H. (2003). Paradigms, citations, and maps of science: A personal history. *Journal of the American Society for Information Science and Technology, 54,* 394–399.
Smallwood, S. (2002). 'Professor accused of plagiarism gets to keep her job'. *Chronicle of Higher Education, 48*(36), A14.

Sokolik, M. (2000). Before the horse is out of the barn: Preventing plagiarism. *Writing Across Berkeley, 1*(2). Retrieved 25 April 2002 from http://www-writing.berkeley.edu/wab/1-2-before.htm

Sowden, C. (2005a). Plagiarism and the culture of multilingual students in higher education abroad. *ELT Journal, 59*, 226–233.

Sowden, C. (2005b). Reply to Dilin Liu. *ELT Journal, 59*, 242–243.

Spack, R. (1997). The acquisition of academic literacy in a second language: A longitudinal case study. *Written Communication, 14*, 3–62.

St. John, M. J. (1987). Writing processes of Spanish scientists publishing in English. *English for Specific Purposes, 6*, 113–120.

Stahl, N., & King, J. R. (1991). Using paraphrasing cards to reduce unintentional plagiarism. *Journal of Reading, 34*, 562–563.

Stearns, L. (1992). Copy wrong: Plagiarism, process, property and the law. *California Review of Law, 80*, 513–553. Also published as (1999) In L. Buranen & A. M. Roy (Eds.), *Perspectives on plagiarism and intellectual property in a postmodern world* (pp. 5–17). Albany, NY: State University of New York Press.

Stoll, L., & Fink, D. (1996). *Changing our schools*. Buckingham: Open University Press.

Susskind, A. (2006, 23 November). Plagiarism rises amid funding cuts. *Sydney Morning Herald*. Retrieved 29 September 2007 from http://www.smh.com.au/news/opinion/plagiarism-rises-amid-funding-cuts/2006/11/22/1163871480372. html?page=fullpage#

Swales, J. M. (1981). *Aspects of Article Introductions*. Aston ESP Research Reports. Birmingham: The University of Aston Language Studies Unit.

Swales, J. M. (1986). Citation analysis and discourse analysis. *Applied Linguistics, 7,* 39–56.

Swales, J. M. (1990). *Genre analysis: English in academic and research settings*. Cambridge: Cambridge University Press.

Swales, J. M. (1996). Occluded genres in the academy: The case of the submission letter. In E. Ventola & A. Mauranen (Eds.), *Academic writing: Intercultural and textual issues* (pp. 45–58). Amsterdam: John Benjamins.

Swales, J. M. (2004). *Research genres: Exploration and applications*. Cambridge: Cambridge University Press.

Swales, J. M., & Feak, C. B. (2004). *Academic writing for graduate students: Essential tasks and skills* (2nd ed.). Ann Arbor, MI: University of Michigan Press.

Swearingen, C. J. (1999). Originality, authenticity, imitation, and plagiarism: Augustine's Chinese cousins. In L. Buranen & A. M. Roy (Eds.), *Perspectives on plagiarism and intellectual property in a postmodern world* (pp. 19–30). Albany, NY: State University of New York Press.

Swinbanks, D. (1993). Survey battle leads to plagiarism verdict. *Nature, 366,* 715.
Tadros, A. (1993). The pragmatics of text averral and attribution in academic texts. In M. Hoey (Ed.), *Data, description, discourse* (pp. 98–114). London: Harper Collins.
Tadros, A. (1994). Predictive categories in expository text. In M. Coulthard (Ed.), *Advances in written text analysis* (pp. 69–82). London and New York: Routledge.
Taylor, L. (1990). *Teaching and learning vocabulary.* New York & London: Prentice Hall.
Taylor, S. J., & Bogdan, R. (1998). *Introduction to qualitative research methods: A guidebook and resource* (3rd ed.). New York: Wiley.
Teitell, C. (1987, 21 September). Was Biden an echo? *New York Times,* p. A19.
Thompson, G., & Ye, Y. (1991). Evaluation of the reporting verbs used in academic papers. *Applied Linguistics, 12,* 365–382.
Thompson, P. (2000). Citation practices in PhD theses. In L. Burnard & T. McEnery (Eds.), *Rethinking language pedagogy from a corpus perspective: Papers from the third international conference on Teaching and Language Corpora.* Frankfurt: Peter Lang.
Thompson, P. (2005). Points of focus and position: Intertextual reference in PhD theses. *Journal of English for Academic Purposes, 4,* 307–323.
Thompson, P., & Tribble, C. (2001). Looking at citations: Using corpora in English for academic purposes. *Language Learning and Technology, 5*(3), 91–105.
Timm, A. (2007a, 5–7 September). *Educational practices at undergraduate level in Greece.* Paper presented at the International Students, Academic Writing and Plagiarism Conference, Lancaster University.
Timm, A. (2007b, 5–7 September). *Educational practices at undergraduate level in India.* Paper presented at the International Students, Academic Writing and Plagiarism Conference, Lancaster University.
Todd, E. S. (1997). Supervising overseas students: Problem or opportunity? In D. McNamara & R. Harris (Eds.), *Overseas students in higher education: Issues in teaching and learning* (pp. 173–186). London: Routledge.
Tralau, J. (2005a). Svar: Är kopierande comme-il-faut? *Axess, 8.* Retrieved 29 June 2007 from http://www.axess.se/svenska/2005/08/debatt_tralau.php
Tralau, J. (2005b, 15 October). Här är ju ännu fler plagiat, Tiina. *Expressen.* Retrieved 29 June 2007 from http://www.expressen.se/1.263055

Truss, L. (2003). *Eats, shoots and leaves: The zero tolerance approach to punctuation.* London: Profile.

Turkish scientists face accusation of plagiarism. (2007, 6 September). *Nature, 449,* 8.

Turrell, T. (2004). Textual kidnapping revisited: The case of plagiarism in literary translation. *International Journal of Speech, Language and the Law, 11,* 1–26.

Ventola, E. (1992). Writing scientific English: Overcoming intercultural problems. *International Journal of Applied Linguistics, 2,* 191–220.

Verma, G. K., & Beard, R. M. (1981). *What is educational research? Perspectives on techniques of research.* Aldershot, Hants: Gower.

Villalva, K. E. (2006). Hidden literacies and inquiry approaches of bilingual high school writers. *Written Communication, 23,* 91–129.

Voorrips, R. E., Jongerius, M.C., & Kanne, H. J. (1997). Mapping of two genes for resistance to clubroot (*Plasmodiophora brassicae*) in a population of doubled haploid lines of *Brassica oleracea* by means of RFLP and AFLP markers. *Theoretical and Applied Genetics, 94,* 75–82.

Wasley, P. (2007). Ohio U. revokes degree for plagiarism. *Chronicle of Higher Education, 53*(31), 10.

Watkins, C. (1985). Does pastoral care = personal and social education? *Pastoral Care, 3*(3), 179–183.

Weissberg, R., & Buker, S. (1990). *Writing up research: Experimental research writing for students of English.* Englewood Cliffs, NJ: Prentice Hall.

Whitaker, E. E. (1993). A pedagogy to address plagiarism. *College Composition and Communication, 44,* 509–514.

White, H. D. (2004). Citation analysis and discourse analysis revisited. *Applied Linguistics, 25,* 89–116.

Wilhoit, S. (1994). Helping students avoid plagiarism. *College Teaching, 42,* 161–164.

Williams, R., & Dallas, D. (1984). Aspects of vocabulary in the readability of content area L2 educational textbooks: A case study. In J. C. Alderson & A. H. Urquhart (Eds.), *Reading in a foreign language.* London and New York: Longman.

Wise, J. E., Nordberg, R. B., & Reitz, D. J. (1967). *Methods of research in education.* Boston: Heath.

Withers, L. A. (1991). Maintenance of plant tissue cultures. In B. E. Kirsop & A. Doyle (Eds.), *Maintenance of microorganisms and cultured cells: A manual of laboratory methods* (2nd ed., pp. 243–267). London: Academic.

Woodmansee, M., & Jaszi, P. (1995). The law of texts: Copyright in the academy. *College English, 57,* 769–787.

Wray, A. (2002). *Formulaic language and the lexicon*. Cambridge: Cambridge University Press.
Yancey, K. B. & Spooner, M. (1998). A single good mind: Collaboration, cooperation, and the writing self. *College Composition and Communication, 49,* 45–62.
Yilmaz, I. (2007, 11 October). Plagiarism? No, we're just borrowing better English. *Nature, 449,* 658.
Zarpetea-Ioannou, M. (1998, March). *Paraphrase: Minus plagiarism, plus language building*. Paper presented at the meeting of IATEFL.
Zebroski, J.T. (1999). Intellectual property, authority, and social formation: Sociohistoricist perspectives on the author function. In L. Buranen & A. M. Roy (Eds.), *Perspectives on plagiarism and intellectual property in a postmodern world* (pp. 31–39). Albany, NY: State University of New York Press.

Author Index

Abasi 97, 138
Ackerman 50
Akbari 97, 138
Akhtar 47, 48
Allen 41
American Psychological
  Association 147
Anderson 55
Angélil-Carter 3, 11, 79, 105
Austin 158

Ballard 50, 150
Barks 20, 36n. 1
Baron 11, 12
Baty 38, 163, 164
Bazerman 175
Becher 41
Becher & Trowler 41, 42
Belcher 22, 50, 51, 159
Berkenkotter 43, 50
Best 66, 67, 107, 108
Betts 2
Biber 69
Biggs 146
Biglan 174
Bjerrum 63
Black 79
Bloch 15, 19, 20, 21, 36n. 1, 159
Bogdan 189
Bowden 150
Bower 186
Braine 8n. 2
Brannen 187–9
Brenner 63, 77

Brogan 13
Broughton 134
Brown 158
Buker 47
Buranen 14, 21, 36n. 1, 149,
  165, 166
Burton 41
Burtonwood 74, 75

Cammish 36n. 1
Campbell 15
Chandrasoma 21
Charles 46, 49, 55n. 4
Chi 15, 20
Clanchy 50, 150
Connor 8n. 2
Cook 165
Cooper 115–16
Cosgrove 170n. 3
Coulthard 98n. 3
Cozzens 41
Crehan 75, 76
Crocker 8n. 2
Cronin 42
Cunningsworth 121
Currie 9, 20, 102

Damich 27
Datta 64
Deckert 10, 17, 18, 19, 36n. 1
DeGroot 158
Dionne 23–7, 28
Dong 8n. 2, 42, 51, 122
Dowd 23, 24, 28

AUTHOR INDEX

Dryden 19, 36n. 1
Dubois 46
Dysthe 51

Erman 168
Errey 10, 14, 61, 105, 156
Faure 130, 131
Feak 46, 147
Fielding 188
Flower 85
Flowerdew 20, 81, 156, 157
Fontana 187
Force 170n. 3
Frey 187
Friedman 170

Gardner 31
Garrow 30, 34
Geisler 87
Giamatti 27
Gibaldi 147
Gilbert 41, 42
Glod 155
Gosden 122
Grimmett 76
Groom 47, 88
Gunnarsson 39

Ha 14
Halbert 11
Hanania 47, 48
Harrison 39
Harwood 42, 50
Hayes 10, 16, 18, 20, 153
Hewings 96–7
Higham 30
Houghton 96–7
Howard 5, 11, 15, 16, 20, 36n. 5, 38, 63, 79, 105, 153, 166, 171
Huckin 43
Hull 165
Hunston 46
Hyland 46, 55n. 2, 164

Introna 10, 16, 18, 20, 153, 170n. 1
Ivanič 112

Jacoby 43, 44
Jaszi 12
Johnson 76
Jullien 170n. 3

Kantz 148
Kaplan 41
Kebler 41
Kennard 118–19
Kirkland 148
Klein 2
Kobayashi 16, 17, 19
Kolich 150
Kramer 8n. 2
Krase 51
Kroll 18
Kvale 189

Lagercrantz 119
Lakoff 76
Larochelle 159
Lawson 92–4, 103
Lave 51, 52
Leatherman 39–40
Lee 187, 189
Leki 8n. 2
Levelt 67
Li 20, 81, 156
Lipetz 42
Liu 14
LoCastro 19
Lovell 92–4, 103

McClanahan 8n. 2
McCracken 170n. 3
McKnight 35
Maher 107–8
Marsh 186
Martin Luther King Jr. Papers Project 29, 32

Masuko 19
Matalene 3, 10
May 25–6
Meislin 25
Midgely 158
Miller 30–3
Moravcsik 42
Murphy 149
Murray 165
Murugesan 42
Myers 47

Nelson 51
Nienhuis 148
Nunan 106
Nunberg 87, 98n. 3

Oakley 80

Palmer 68, 69, 91
Pecorari 8n. 2, 16, 38, 46, 52, 73, 152
Pennycook 12, 21
Petrić 8n. 2, 49, 150
Pickard 46
Popham 69–72, 103
Porter 158
Price 40–1
Prior 8n. 2
Pulgram 95–6
Pyle 110–11

Rogen 1, 27
Raines 23
Ramsay 109–10
Randall 170n. 3
Reagon 33
Renzetti 187, 189
Rheem 27
Richards 87
Rinnert 16, 17, 19
Roig 20, 38, 61, 115, 156
Rose 165
Rubin 179, 187

Safire 25
St. John 8n. 2
Salager-Meyer 43, 46, 175
San Miguel 51
Sapp 36n. 1
Saunders 148
Sciolino 170n. 3
Scollon 12
Shadish 41
Shaw 8n. 2, 48, 52
Sherman 8n. 2, 148
Shi 15, 19–20
Shibata 41
Sieber 187
Simmons 158
Sinclair 53
Small 40–2
Smallwood 40
Sowden 14, 36n. 1
Spack 8n. 2
Stahl 148
Stearns 55n. 1
Stoll 67, 79, 80
Susskind 163
Swales 42–4, 46, 55nn. 4, 5
Swinbanks 39

Tadros 43, 47, 85
Taylor 189
Teitell 25
Thompson, G. 41, 44
Thompson, P. 43, 46, 48, 50, 55n. 3
Timm 20, 122
Todd 36n. 1
Tralau 39
Tribble 43, 46, 47, 50
Truss 87
Turrell 98n. 2

Ventola 122
Verma 63, 80, 91, 181, 182
Villalva 111, 167
Voorrips 140, 141

Warren 168
Wasley 38
Watkins 78
Watts 20, 36n. 1
Weissberg 47
Wenger 51, 52
Whitaker 148, 149
White 41–2
Wilhoit 148, 149
Williams 128

Wise 168
Withers 62, 181
Woodmansee 12
Wray 69, 167, 168, 169

Ye 41, 44, 45

Zarpetea-Ioannou 148
Zebroski 159

Subject Index

African American folk pulpit 30
apprenticeship 50–4
attribution 4, 6, 23, 34, 35, 26, 27, 29, 53, 54, 63, 65, 81, 91, 139, 156, 161, 181
averral 53–4, 91

Biden, Joseph 23–9, 34, 35, 36n. 4

cheating 10, 14, 18, 100, 101, 135, 146
citation
  author prominent 47, 92
  co-citation 40
  information-prominent 47
  integral 43–7, 55n. 4
  non-integral 43–7
  secondary 29, 73, 75, 77, 79, 117, 179, 188
citation forms
  in-text 43, 55n. 4
  end notes 44
  footnotes 43
citer motivation 41
conventions
  for source use 77, 105, 113, 116, 132, 134, 150, 166, 169, 175, 178–80, 189
copyright 11–12, 159
create a research space (CARS) model 42
cryptomnesia 186
culture
  plagiarism and 12–22, 35

detecting plagiarism 58–9, 125, 136–7, 145, 149, 170n. 1, 189
electronic detection 2, 146, 151, 153, 155, 170n. 1, 183
disciplines, academic 20, 42, 46, 49, 50, 55n. 3, 62, 98n. 2, 125, 142, 147, 150, 164, 174, 179, 188
  hard 46–9, 55n. 3, 62, 105, 174
  soft 46–9, 55n. 3, 62, 174
disciplinary measures 6, 38–9, 151, 158, 186, 188
discourse communities 1, 5, 6, 7, 17, 20, 29, 30, 33, 35, 49, 52, 112, 122, 159, 164

educational system
  role of in teaching source use 19
endnotes see citation form
Enlightenment 11

footnotes see citation form
formulaic language 69, 111–12, 167–9

genre 33, 35, 37, 46, 55n. 5, 164
Google 68–9, 98n. 3, 160

information science 40–1
intellectual property 11, 19, 27
intention to deceive 4–6, 10, 26, 32, 81, 99–105, 113, 131, 133–6, 152, 156, 169, 180, 186

SUBJECT INDEX

international students 12–22, 35, 157, 162, 172–5
internet 9, 148, 154–5, 158–62, 164
in-text references *see* citation form

King, Martin Luther, Jr. 29–35
Kinnock, Neil 22–8, 31, 36nn. 2, 4

language chunks *see* formulaic language
legitimate peripheral participation 51–4, 148

occlusion 53–5, 55n. 5, 60, 123, 136–7, 148

'paper mills' 154, 158
paraphrase 4, 20, 29, 39, 43, 53, 54, 55n. 2, 60, 75, 78, 94, 105, 106, 108, 109, 112–16, 121, 122, 132, 148, 166, 179
patchwriting 5, 9, 20, 63, 105–6, 110, 111, 123, 137, 145, 146, 151–3, 165–6, 169, 171, 186
plagiarism
    as a sensitive research topic 142, 187–90
    as theft 1, 11, 27, 37, 128, 142
    attitudes toward 1–3
    causes of 13–22, 35, 105–21
    cultural attitudes toward *see* culture
    deceptive *see* intention to deceive
    definitions of 1, 4–6, 38
    disagreement about 10, 35, 38, 40, 135, 143, 157

metaphors for 1, 11, 27, 37, 128, 142
penalties for 34, 37, 146, 169, 187
prototypical 4–5, 9, 99, 135, 145, 146, 149, 151, 171
    textual 4–6, 10, 13, 16, 18, 20, 21, 29–30, 33, 35, 58, 61, 82, 96, 98, 99, 105, 120, 123, 143, 145, 146, 149–56, 163, 166, 169, 182
policies
    plagiarism 37–8, 116, 151, 152
political discourse
    plagiarism in 22–9, 31, 36n. 3
prototypical plagiarism *see* plagiarism
public cases 22–36, 39–40, 163–4

quotation *see* form of incorporation

reporting forms 43–9, 55n. 2, 93, 134, 147, 179

secondary citation *see* citation
sociology of science 40–4
source use
    opaque 61–81, 73, 75, 77, 104, 123, 125, 127, 138
    transparent 60, 61–82, 98, 104, 146, 147, 149, 154, 155
Stationers' Guild 11
Statute of Queen Anne 12
style manuals 147

textual plagiarism *see* plagiarism

writing, second-language 9, 97